JOHN DEAR
on
PEACE

An Introduction to His Life and Work

PATRICIA PATTEN NORMILE, S.F.O.

ST. ANTHONY MESSENGER PRESS
Cincinnati, Ohio

LIBRARY OF CONGRESS CATALOGING-IN-PUBLICATION DATA
Normile, Patricia Patten.
John Dear on peace : an introduction to his life and work / Patricia Patten Normile.
p. cm.
Includes bibliographical references (p.   ) and index.
ISBN 978-0-86716-854-9 (pbk. : alk. paper) 1. Dear, John, 1959- 2. Peace—Religious aspects—Catholic Church. I. Title.
BX1795.P43N676 2009
241'.6242—dc22
2008047465

ISBN 978-0-86716-854-9

Published by St. Anthony Messenger Press
28 W. Liberty St.
Cincinnati, OH 45202
www.SAMPBooks.org

Printed in the United States of America.

Printed on acid-free paper.

09 10 11 12 13 5 4 3 2 1

contents

Vow of Nonviolence

Recognizing the violence in my own heart, yet trusting in the goodness and mercy of God, I vow to practice the nonviolence of Jesus who taught us in the Sermon on the Mount—

"Blessed are the peacemakers, they will be called the sons and daughters of God.... You have heard that it was said, love your neighbor and hate your enemy. But I say to you, Love your enemies and pray for those who persecute you that you may be sons and daughters of your God in heaven."

Before God the Creator and the Holy Spirit, I vow to carry out in my life the love and example of Jesus

—by striving for peace within myself and seeking to be a peace maker in my daily life;
—by accepting suffering in the struggle for justice rather than inflicting it;
—by refusing to retaliate in the face of provocation and violence;
—by persevering in nonviolence of tongue and heart;
—by living conscientiously and simply so that I do not deprive others of the means to live or harm creation;
  by actively resisting evil and working nonviolently to abolish war and the causes of war from my own heart and from the face of the earth.

God, I trust in your sustaining love and believe that just as you gave me the grace and desire to offer this, so you will also bestow abundant grace to fulfill it.

introduction

*A*s I began writing this book, the thought flashed across my mind, "Wouldn't it be wonderful if by the time this work is finished, it would be a totally unnecessary book? Wars around the globe would have ceased forever. Families, colleagues in the workplace, kids on the playgrounds, motorists on the highways, neighbors and friends encountering misunderstandings all would be working toward harmony on matters where opinions diverge." Of course, the message of history tells us that will most likely not be the situation in the world any time soon. Perhaps my grandmother's wisdom applies here. During the winter of her ninetieth year, she perused a garden catalog, making selections of bushes and plants she planned to purchase, some of which would not mature or bloom for several years. Maybe she read my mind as I mentally questioned whether in her weakened condition she would live long enough to delight in these plantings. She said with a smile, "I may not be around to enjoy these plants, but you, your children and others will be. That's what matters—making the world a more beautiful place."

Peace may not rise from the ashes of the world's wars as soon as we hope and pray it will. Nevertheless, we work for peace one day at a time for those future generations toddling around today with the innocence of the young and for all who nurture hope and love in their hearts. We also pray that those who do not harbor a longing for peace with loving and hopeful hearts may be converted to desire peace.

On September 11, 2001, I sat with our almost one-year-old granddaughter cuddled in my lap for her morning nap. Our son, Dan, called to relay to me the events striking America in New York, Washington, D.C., and the fields of Pennsylvania. I turned the television on but muted it. Dan kept reminding me not to let little Ellie see the scenes of devastation. I stifled my outcry into a deep moan as the second plane hit in New York. Amid the anguish of the moment as it soon became apparent that these were deliberate attacks, one thought kept surfacing, "I will not hate these people!" I silently repeated those words to myself over and over. Who these people were was an unknown in those moments but I knew that my hatred would only add to the hatred in the world that would allow such acts of terror to be committed. I vowed not to hate.

The next morning I went to Mass at a retreat center near our home. As I entered the small chapel before Mass, I heard one daily communicant almost shouting, "Kill 'em! Kill 'em! Just kill 'em all!" The statement was an astonishing, vehement profession of hatred coming from a believer in Jesus, the Prince of Peace. I entered the chapel and quietly asked, "Who are 'them'?" No answer. Silence followed until Mass commenced.

Those mornings remain ingrained in my brain. My resolve not to hate in the face of hatred remains, as does the sadness that there are those who conjure up such a hatred for our country, our people, our way of life and our faith that they would destroy thousands of innocents. Sadness also remains that there are others who desire vengeance and retaliation to be hurled against other innocents. Certainly we were all devastated by the events of 9/11 as we sought to comprehend what had taken place. I pondered how our Catholic Christian faith could keep us following in the ways of Jesus amid the anger, pain and loss of a way of life that we had lived in relative security.

As months went on, another event heightened my deep desire for peace. As I watched the evening news, I saw an Iraqi father in Baghdad running for safety amid heavy shelling. Gathered in his arms was a beautiful toddler who looked over his shoulder with incredible terror in her eyes. She looked exactly like our granddaughter, Ellie, whom I had held that fateful September morning. That image, which lingers in my heart, links me in an ever-deepening way to the need for peace in our everyday lives. It reminds me that every child, indeed, every person, is beloved of other humans and of God who created them.

My resolve for peace remains though I have been verbally assaulted along the way by those who felt retaliation was the only way to react to the events of 9/11 and other occasions of hostility. I still hear echoes of the "Kill 'em all!" mentality. Yet others agree that on September 12, 2001, the day after, the U.S. in its deep grief had a perfect opportunity to gather the world community of peace-seeking nations into a powerful instrument of peace. Of course, the perpetrators behind the hideous attacks needed to be sought and brought to justice, but spawning another war seems a strange way to establish peace.

A passage from the Hebrew Scriptures seemed to speak to me: "...if my people who are called by my name humble themselves, pray, seek my face, and turn from their wicked ways, then I will hear from heaven, and will forgive their sin and heal their land" (2 Chronicles 7:14). I sent that verse of Scripture to dozens of people because it had caused me to look at myself, my country, my culture from a different perspective. Why would others hate us so much as to blast innocent people with such heinous acts of terrorism? Does our culture have evil, wicked ways? Most assuredly. Simply flip through the television channels and you will find your spirit assaulted by violence, greed, gross sexuality and ungodliness in many forms. I am a patriotic American. I love the United States of America. That love makes me want more for this country than a degraded sense of "freedom." I was a child of war; my dad landed on Omaha Beach (thankfully not on D-Day but days later) and marched across France with General Patton's army. I respect the sacrifices made by that Greatest Generation. Yet, like a parent who loves a child and would not want to see that child pursue destructive ways, I long to see the U.S. turn from wars of retaliation, the stockpiling of nuclear armaments, support of violent governments and to expand its role in feeding the hungry, housing the homeless, training the unemployed, providing healthcare for the sick. We live in an era when the next war may well be the last war because of the monstrous ability of nuclear warheads to destroy the earth.

Many questions continue to haunt me. How can one be an instrument of peace in a world bent on war? How can one "turn the other cheek" when struck with such hateful force as in the 9/11 attacks? Through my ponderings, I keep remembering Jesus' words in the Garden of Gethsemane, "Put down the sword!" and again as he appeared to his followers after the Resurrection, "Peace be with you." Jesus wasn't joking! He sincerely meant those words, as difficult as they may seem to live out in our everyday lives.

As I struggled with the meaning of all the conflict, suffering and uncertainty that have entered our lives, I met the peace activist John Dear, S.J.

And that's where this book begins.

John and I have served on the board of directors of the San Damiano Foundation. This foundation was established by Gerard

Thomas Straub in 2002 to support efforts to film the plight of the abjectly poor around the world and the work of those who strive to alleviate their pain and suffering. Gerry is the former Hollywood producer of the popular shows *General Hospital* and *The Doctors*. Gerry enjoyed his former work and the great wealth it brought his way. He claims that during this period of his life he had rejected his early Catholic upbringing and became an atheist. But that was not God's plan for Gerry.

Gerry left the world of television after becoming disgruntled at the quality of programming that was being produced. One TV executive told Gerry that his problem was that he wanted to be an artist in his trade but what the network wanted was "filler" to keep the commercials from bumping together.

In 1995, Gerry traveled to Europe in an attempt to complete a novel about the beloved peace activist Saint Francis of Assisi and the artist Vincent Van Gogh that he had been working on for several years. He hoped by walking in their footsteps he could find a way to complete his book. Instead, he found himself in an empty church in Rome, weeping as he read Psalm 63, "O God, you are my God, I seek you, / my soul thirsts for you...." (63:1). This psalm was a call from God that touched his heart and profoundly altered his life. Gerry's change of heart prompted him to write *The Sun & Moon Over Assisi*, which has been compared to Thomas Merton's *Seven Storey Mountain* as it probes the depths of spiritual conversion.

The Sun & Moon Over Assisi led to a meeting between John Dear and Gerry Straub. John relates, "We were both guests of our publishers at the invitation-only annual conference for booksellers in the U.S. There were stalls from all the leading publishers. It was Chicago, I think 2001. My book was *Living Peace*, and his was *Sun and Moon*. He had read my book *The Sound of Listening*, about staying in Merton's hermitage, while he was on retreat in Merton's hermitage, and wanted to meet me.... So we talked and talked, then stayed in touch, and then the next thing I knew, he was starting a foundation...."

These two men had found the common bond between them, their desire for God. Their desire for God's justice and their desire for peace are their bonded values. The two became fast friends, and John joined the San Damiano Foundation's board of directors.

I had read some of John Dear's writings on peace and found them to be profoundly pure gospel. John lives and teaches active non-violence. I wanted to know more about how one could actually be a nonviolent person in such a violent world. When I met John at a San Damiano board meeting in early 2006, I began to understand the "how" of living as a person of peace. John simply exudes a sense of peace as he strives to follow the Prince of Peace.

*S*o just who is John Dear? He is an author who has written more than twenty books. John (he says everyone just calls him John) holds two master's degrees in theology from the Graduate Theological Union in California. He has been featured in *The New York Times, The Washington Post, USA Today,* National Public Radio's *All Things Considered, America, U. S. Catholic* and *The National Catholic Reporter.* He served as the director of the Fellowship of Reconciliation, one of the largest interfaith peace organizations in the U.S. John counts among his friends and acquaintances the late Mother Teresa, peace activists Daniel and Philip Berrigan, Nobel Peace Prize–winners Mairead Maguire and Archbishop Desmond Tutu, Bishop Thomas Gumbleton, Thich Nhat Hanh, Martin Sheen, Joan Baez and Sister Helen Prejean, to name a few. In 2008, John was nominated for the Nobel Peace Prize.

John has worked in homeless shelters, soup kitchens and community centers. His travels and work have taken him to war zones of the world including Iraq, Palestine, El Salvador, Guatemala and Northern Ireland. John's present home is on a high mesa in New Mexico. He serves as coordinator of Pax Christi New Mexico and campaigns relentlessly to close the Livermore Laboratories and to disarm Los Alamos, centers of atomic research and production. He crusades for the closure of the Western Hemisphere Institute for Security Cooperation (WHINSEC), formerly known as the School of the Americas (SOA), a U.S. government–operated military training base housed at Ft. Benning, Georgia, where foreign military agents are trained in terrorism. While John's activities are dynamic, his manner is one of gentleness—gentle confidence that springs from his God-confidence.

John is a Jesuit, a scholar, a son, a brother, a friend, a prayer, a priest, an activist and a *felon*. Yes, a felon, a label that stems from his peaceful protests against nuclear arms. He has been arrested more than seventy-five times for acts of civil disobedience in protesting war and nuclear arms. He spent eight months in prison for a Plowshares disarmament action in which he and three companions entered the Seymour Johnson air force base and hammered on an F15E fighter plane with nuclear capabilities. This act was a symbol of the necessity for nuclear disarmament by the U.S. As of this writing, he has given well over a thousand lectures on peace at universities and churches across the country. John is a courageous personification of peace.

On the morning of September 11, 2001, John was to meet his parents for breakfast at Windows on the World atop the World Trade Center. A few nights before, John's mother called him to say she had changed their reservation to another location to make John's morning commute easier. The Dears were at breakfast when the planes struck the World Trade Center. After the attacks, as others fled

Manhattan, John ran toward the city to help where he could. During the post-9/11 days, he served as New York City's Red Cross coordinator of chaplains at the family assistance center, counseling thousands of relatives and friends of the victims, as well as hundreds of rescue workers. He later escorted victims' families to the site of devastation. He personally faced the ravages of violence blasted into the hearts and lives of those afflicted by the event.

Where did John's mission for peace begin? Defining the absolute source of his mission for peace might be difficult but one particular event marked a launch point for his vocation in nonviolence. In his own words John describes that event:

I remember the day I was confronted with my great choice. In June 1982, I was twenty-one, living with my parents in Washington, D.C., about to enter the Society of Jesus, the Jesuits, a worldwide community of Catholic priests. I decided that before I committed my life to following Jesus, I wanted to go to Israel and see for myself the land where Jesus lived and died.

My plans for a typical pious pilgrimage were shattered though. As I was boarding the plane to Tel Aviv, Israel was invading Lebanon. I was heading into a war. Stepping off the plane in Tel Aviv, I was greeted by armed soldiers who searched me, questioned me, and finally waved me on with machine guns.... But the reality of the war shocked me, terrified me, and changed my life.

After exploring every corner of Jerusalem, Bethlehem, and Nazareth, I spent the last week camping out by myself along the Sea of Galilee. It was beautiful. Each morning, I rose with the sun, swam in the cool water, and meditated on the teachings of Jesus, who lived and worked along the north shore of Galilee, in the village of Capernaum.

Every day, I climbed a little hill on the north shore near the ruins of Capernaum to pray in the Chapel of the Beatitudes. The eight-sided chapel is surrounded by palm trees, cactus, and green shrubs. There I would sit in silence and read the words of scripture engraved on the walls. I would walk out onto the balcony and look out at the blue sea. The view was breathtaking. For hours, I would read the Sermon on the Mount, look at the sea , and pray for guidance.

As my time in Galilee drew to a close, I made one last visit to the Chapel of the Beatitudes. I sat alone in the chapel reading the words written on the eight windows:

> *Blessed are the poor in spirit. Theirs is the reign of heaven.*
>
> *Blessed are those who mourn. They shall be comforted.*
>
> *Blessed are the meek. They shall inherit the land.*
>
> *Blessed are those who hunger and thirst for justice. They shall be satisfied.*
>
> *Blessed are the merciful. They shall be shown mercy.*
>
> *Blessed are the pure in heart. They shall see God.*
>
> *Blessed are the peacemakers. They shall be called sons and daughters of God.*
>
> *Blessed are those who are persecuted for the sake of justice. Theirs is the reign of heaven.*
>
> *Blessed are you when others revile you and persecute you and utter all kinds of evil against you falsely on my account. Rejoice and be glad, for your reward is great in heaven. (Matthew 5:3–12)*

"I say to you, love your enemies, and pray for those who persecute you, that you may be children of your heavenly God, for God makes God's sun rise on the bad and the good, and causes rain to fall on the just and the unjust. Be compassionate as your heavenly God is compassionate." (Matthew 5:44–45)

Suddenly, the words of Jesus hit me as if for the first time. As a light went on, I thought to myself, *Oh my God, I think he's serious!*

I walked onto the balcony and looked out at the sea, the distant mountains, the clear blue sky.

"Are you trying to tell me something, God?" I said aloud, looking up at the sky. "Do you want even me to become a peacemaker, to hunger and thirst for justice, to love my enemies?

"Okay, God," I said out loud. "I promise to live the life of peace, to live out these Beatitudes for the rest of my life—on one condition: if you give me a sign!"

With that, I put my fist down on the stone wall, proud of my conditional commitment.

Just then, two Israeli war jets fell through the sky, breaking the sound barrier with sonic booms, over the Sea of Galilee, flying low, straight toward me! I ducked instinctively. They raced directly over me and the Chapel of the Beatitudes and, seconds later, dropped several bombs along the border between Israel and Lebanon.

I rose and looked back up at the sky.

"Okay, God," I said, shaking. "I promise to dedicate myself to peace and justice for the rest of my life—and I'll never ask for a sign again!"[1]

From this stunning call to peace and with his vast background as an advocate of active nonviolence, how does John Dear describe the mission of peacemakers? The words may seem simple; the challenge arises in living out the task:

Our task, in these dark times, is simple: to speak the truth, resist war and injustice, practice nonviolence, walk with the poor, love everyone, say our prayers, and uphold the vision of a new world without war, poverty or nuclear weapons. We are called to follow the nonviolent Jesus on the road to peace. If we can be faithful to the God of peace and the Way of nonviolence, we will receive the gift of living peace.[2]

The more I read of John's work in his books, papers, columns, the more I realized I had discovered a spiritual guide in a troubled world. I began to think of John as a Jesuit with a Franciscan heart. It also occurred to me that John is such a prolific writer that most people may not take the time to read all his writing and wisdom. An idea began to emerge of creating a book of reflections on various topics related to active nonviolence and peace based on John's work and writing. *John Dear on Peace: An Introduction to His Life and Work* is not intended to capture all that John's writings teach. His writings are far too vast and deep to accomplish that in one volume. This is simply an introduction to an authentic gospel approach to peace, a way of active nonviolence that John lives and invites others to enter. Each reflection leads readers to the books from which the material is taken. Readers are encouraged to read the full text of the books at some time in the future. A reading list appears at the end of this book.

The challenge! As I read and reread John's books, I often found it necessary to stop both the reading and writing of this book. At times the message was simply too astounding and sometimes too painful. At these times I followed the admonition of Saint Francis of Assisi who used to say, "If you are upset for any reason whatever, you should immediately rise up to prayer, and you should remain in the presence of the Most High Father for as long as it takes him to restore you to the joy of your salvation." It worked. Each time I would be able to return to writing, trusting in God's guidance for John and for myself. I recommend the same for you if the truths revealed in John's writings seem overpowering.

Enabling *John Dear on Peace: An Introduction to His Life and Work* to Guide Your Journey

John Dear on Peace is not intended to be a sit-down-and-read-cover-to-cover-book. The reflections do not have to be read and pondered in the order presented. However, beginning with the first three reflections—"What is Peace?," "Living Justly in an Unfair World" and "Resisting Vengeance"—will establish a pattern for reading. After that, you may wish to choose reflections that are particularly pertinent to where your thoughts and feelings of the day may be or what events emblazon the news.

Each reflection focuses on a justice and peace-related concept. Find a quiet place to read the introductory portion of the reflection.

Consider your own views and feelings about the topic.

What in the text about the topic brings you comfort?

What in that same text causes concern and conflict within you?

Ask yourself if you truly desire to have a new outlook regarding the particular topic.

Are you open to new ideas regarding the topic?

You might pray for an open mind and willing spirit to guide your reading and your personal reflection on the topic.

Selections from John Dear's books and writings follow the introduction to each reflection. Read a selected quotation. Ask yourself what the quotation means to you on this particular day. What do you resist in the idea? What do you accept?

Proceed to another quote or simply stay with one for an extended time. You might copy and post the quote in a place where you will see it during the day—in your car, on your desk or the bathroom mirror.

Allow the thought to speak to you. You might share it with a friend. You might find it helpful to keep a journal to record your reactions.

When you have read and considered all the reading selections, ponder the questions.

John Dear on Peace may be used by individuals, book clubs, Scripture study groups or prayer groups. Sharing the readings and reflections with another person or a group opens new ideas for thought, discussion and prayer, allowing the readers to express their impressions and their own struggles with the issues involved. If disagreements arise, opportunity exists to practice peaceful resolve of the differences of opinion.

The hope is that John Dear's messages will move from head to heart to spirit and ultimately to hands and feet as you begin to live out the message of each reflection. You will discover that *John Dear on Peace* is not completely written. The final chapter is yours to write, to write with your life and your personal commitment to Jesus, that you too will follow the way of peace for the rest of your life.

Notes

[1] John Dear, *Living Peace: A Spirituality of Contemplation and Action* (New York: Image, 2001), pp. 75–78.

[2] John Dear, previously unpublished.

What Is Peace?

> ...to set the mind on the Spirit is life and peace.
> —Romans 8:6

*hat is peace? We talk about it.* We mourn its absence. We long for it. We pray for it. As I ponder peace, the words of an old song drift through my mind: "Peace is flowing like a river, flowing out of you and me, flowing out into the desert, setting all the captives free." Peace is that intangible quality or charism that wells within us and flows between individuals and nations, creating bonds of well being, hope and harmony. Peace truly sets us free to be the people God has created us to be. Before peace can bond nations, it must dwell in the hearts and lives of the citizens of the world, binding us together as children of God.

We experience the fragility of peace at a personal level. An adult child makes a foolish choice that damages his life. A driver cuts us off in traffic with no regard for our safety. A friend tells an untruth about us and peace between us is disrupted. Identity theft creates a nightmare of legal and financial problems for us. Such events, minor or major, threaten our sense of peace at least temporarily. The challenge is to have at our disposal the tools of reconciliation for such circumstances in order to move as quickly as possible into a renewed state of peaceful existence as we deal with the ramifications of the event.

The Hebrew word for peace is *shalom*. Shalom denotes peace that is all-encompassing. It is love expressed in concern and compassion for others. It swaddles our thoughts and deeds. Shalom might be thought of as the breath of the soul, bringing life and joy to our existence. Shalom can exist in circumstances that seem to render it impossible. We hear of that shalom when individuals who are threatened by unspeakable horror experience and exhibit the peace that passes all understanding.

Jesus does not seem specifically to have defined "peace" to his disciples. Instead, he lives it. He bestows it upon them again and again but not with a "peace is…" defining connotation. He eats with unacceptable folks. He heals people. He challenges the authorities. By these actions Jesus shows ways leading to living peace. Each of us must search for the meaning of peace. As Jesus wishes peace to others, that peace is frequently coupled with "grace." Therefore, peace appears to be a gift of grace to those who follow him. The inference is that you can't have one without the other. Also implied in this juxtaposition of words is that by accepting this gift of grace, peace is possible in our lives—not only possible but demanded of us. Jesus' offering of peace often comes as a kind of command. "Peace I leave with you" does not seem to be an option. Refusing what Jesus presents to us seems unconscionable. Yet we do refuse that gift each time we act or react in violence, unjust anger or in retaliation.

Our church wished to use the song, "Let There Be Peace on Earth," by Sy Miller and Jill Jackson in a service we were preparing. The words "Let there be peace on earth, and let it begin with me" particularly spoke to our peace theme. We phoned the creators of the song for the required permission to reprint the words and music. Their generous response was enthusiastic. "Use it whenever and wherever you wish! Peace must begin with us!" Jill Jackson declared. Indeed, peace must begin with each of us. Take a few moments to consider your concept of peace. What ideas can you add to the following thoughts? If you are keeping a peace journal, you might begin by jotting down your vision of peace.

Peace is infinitely more than an absence of conflict.

Peace is a state of being in any and all circumstances.

Peace is a life merged in the way of Jesus.

Peace is fragile.

Peace is gentle.

Peace is strong and powerful.

Peace is eternal.

Peace is elusive yet always present if we but seek it.

Peace is God's freely given gift.

Peace is spiritual, physical, mental.

Peace is attainable.

Peace is mine to give.

Peace is yours to receive.

Peace is found in silence.

Peace is hope.

Peace is present in pandemonium.

Peace is external

Peace is internal.

Peace is practical.

Peace is shalom.

Peace. It does not mean to be in a place where there is no noise, no trouble or hard work. It means to be in the midst of those things and still be calm in your heart.[1]

John Dear offers us the following thoughts about the meaning of peace in our lives. Consider them. If you find yourself disagreeing with a statement, ask what troubles you about that thought. If a particular statement resonates with you, leading you to want to embody it into your life, write it and post it in a place where you will see it often. Make it your prayer for yourself and for the world.

thoughts from john

Peace is the ongoing celebration of life.[2]

Peace begins within each of us. It is a process of repeatedly showing mercy to ourselves, forgiving ourselves, befriending ourselves, accepting ourselves, and loving ourselves. As we learn to appreciate ourselves and accept God's gift of peace, we begin to radiate peace and love to others.[3]

Every moment offers us God's invitation to live in God's own peace. Wherever we are, we can reject violence and war, and take up the exciting journey by proclaiming God's reign of peace here on earth.[4]

As we choose a life of peace, we end the wars raging within our own hearts and root out every trace of violence. We let go of violent language, habits, manners, and jobs, and cease whatever actions, however subtle, that hurt or threaten others.[5]

Nothing can be more beautiful than living peace.[6]

As we try to live out God's peace in our lives, and turn to God in quiet prayer, we can hear an inner voice, the voice of God, whisper: "Come to me and draw from the springs of peace. Seek peace and you will find peace. Be merciful and you will find mercy. Where there is no love, put love and you will find love."[7]

reflection questions

1. Describe a time in your life when you have felt most at peace.
2. What circumstances rob you of your sense of peace?
3. How can you take steps to live peace?
4. How can you recapture and claim the peace that passes all understanding when it seems absent?

scripture to ponder

O LORD, you will ordain peace for us,
  for indeed, all that we have done, you have done for us. (Isaiah 26:12)

Now may the Lord of peace himself give you peace at all times in all ways. The Lord be with all of you. (2 Thessalonians 3:16)

Grace to you and peace from God our Father and the Lord Jesus Christ. (Philemon 1:3)

I [Paul] therefore, ...beg you to lead a life worthy of the calling to which you have been called, with all humility and gentleness, with patience, bearing with one another in love, making every effort to maintain the unity of the Spirit in the bond of peace. (Ephesians 4:1–3)

concluding prayer

I pray, God, that you will continue to be with me and help me to grow in awareness of your constant abiding presence. Send your Spirit of life down on me, take pity on me, and give me strength for the days ahead as I try to walk with your people. Dear God, I love you. I'm very weak and very frail and I'm trying to do so many things for your people, for your reign of justice and peace. I let go of my cares and anxieties; I offer you my future and my very life that you might use me to serve your suffering people and to help transform our world into a place of justice, peace and love. I ask your blessing on me and on every human being in the world. I let go of everything and pray for a spirit of emptiness, compassion and love that I may be Jesus present in the world. Jesus, you are the whole reason for living and being and acting. Everything I'm doing is for you, with you, through you, because of you. I am yours. I am trying to be your follower, your disciple, here and now. Come, be with me and show me how I can love as you loved, serve as you serve, speak as you speak, love others as you love everyone. O God, make me an instrument of your peace.[8] Amen.

Notes

1 Anonymous.
2 *Living Peace,* p. 110.
3 *Living Peace,* p. 10.
4 *Living Peace,* p. 79.
5 *Living Peace,* p. 83.
6 *Living Peace,* p. 224.
7 John Dear, *Seeds of Nonviolence* (Baltimore: Fortkamp, 1992), p. 332.
8 *Seeds of Nonviolence,* pp. 27–28.

reflection two

Living Justly in an Unjust World

If we confess our sins, he who is faithful and just will forgive
us our sins and cleanse us from all unrighteousness.

—1 John 1:9

*T*hrough the years we hear stories
of individuals and groups who rise from situations of intense pain
and suffering inflicted unjustly and yet still exhibit astonishing forgiveness and compassion. When a gunman broke into an Amish
school in Pennsylvania in 2006, killing five girls and injuring others,
the message that the community sent into the world was one of
unconditional forgiveness. The bereaved people wanted the outside
community to know that they forgave the killer of their children.
They went giant steps further as they reached out with compassion
to the man's wife and three children. They offered prayers and
financial support to that bereft family who had lost their husband
and father when he took his own life. Members of the Amish community even attended the killer's funeral.

"How could they do that?" many queried. Hearing the news accounts of the killings wrenched the hearts of people around the world, often creating an instant desire for some sort of revenge. But the faithful of the Amish community knew that vengeance and retaliation or hatred would only scar their already torn and aching hearts more deeply. At a time of life's greatest challenge they responded with words and actions that revealed their deep faith. In their pain, they taught the world a vital lesson of how to live justly in an unfair world.

In the 1980s in Bellavista Prison, the most violent prison in Colombia, an ex-con made an amazing proposal. A new Christian and former inmate, Oscar Osorio, asked the warden's permission to begin Bible studies among the prisoners. Many of the inmates were professional assassins involved in the drug trade, as well as political and social disputes. Violence within the prison walls was rampant. Approximately 15 percent of the six hundred inmates died violently within the prison each year. The warden agreed reluctantly because no volunteers were permitted inside the prison. No guarantee could be given for Osorio's safety. Osorio's initial twelve-hour days within the cellblocks were spent praying with inmates and teaching them the Bible's message. Not all was pleasant for him. He was greeted with threats to his life, pelted with eggs, garbage and urine, but he refused to give up.

Gradually the flock of the faithful grew within the prison. Then riots broke out. Officials pondered calling in the military to quell the riots, a move that would surely have resulted in a bloodbath. Osorio offered a different approach, which was accepted. Christian prisoners met for prayer in the early morning and began a fast. They moved through the prison preaching in the various cellblocks. One inmate who witnessed savage brutality said, "We kept praying and fasting. We went through every hallway, asking God to take over this jail." The prison was transformed. Subsequently, the Bellavista

Bible Institute was established within the prison. Oscar Osorio, a man who had lived unjustly in the world, found a new way to live in faith and peace and brought that way into the hostile confines of the death culture of a prison.

Reginald Denny barely survived the severe beating he experienced during the 1992 Los Angeles riots spurred by the verdict in the Rodney King police brutality case. Denny met his attackers in the courtroom. Their mothers were there, too. Denny offered a handshake and then hugs to the two women. Looking at their sons, his attackers, he realized, "...when I saw them sitting there, they are not the bad guys they probably appear to be on the street." Embracing the mothers, searching for goodness in his assailants, Denny discovered a way to live justly in an unjust world.

Seeking justice in an unjust world is preliminary to achieving peace. Families must have food and housing. Children need education. All people require adequate healthcare. Adults must have opportunities for work to provide for themselves and their families. The elderly must be cared for when no longer able to care for themselves. When these elements of justice are absent, frustration, pain and anger explode into violent situations. Working for an equitable world in which preferential treatment is given to the poor because they have fewer resources to care for themselves is Jesus' way.

Doctor Tony Lazzara was a pediatrician in Florida when he heard of the critical lack of medical care for children in Peru. Decades ago he moved to Peru and established a hospital to care for children brought to him from the poorest areas of the region. Many of the children lived with him while receiving treatment. Volunteers heard of his work and have come to help care for the children. Justice bloomed for these sick little ones because Doctor Tony saw the need and responded with love and acted with justice.

In these accounts of forgiveness and working for justice in the wake of great suffering we find people doing what Jesus would do: forgiving their assailants and caring for those in need. "Do what Jesus would do" is our call if we bear the name Christian.

What is it we are looking for in our lives? A good place to begin our daily meditation is to sit in silent peace with the holy desires within us, and to imagine Jesus looking at us with loving kindness and asking, "What are you looking for?"

What would we say to Jesus? As we look at him, as we feel his sincerity and love, and as we notice his lack of judgment or anger, we can let those deep desires surface and be spoken. Seeing the love in his eyes, we know that he will not laugh at or reject us. We know that the best within us comes from God, that God has given us everything that is holy within us, and that he will affirm whatever holy desires we seek.[1]

Jesus told the crowds that they had to learn for themselves to judge right from wrong. Today his teachings sound like kindergarten lessons, but true spiritual wisdom is so simple that children grasp it better than adults. Love one another, Jesus said over and over again, and when you fail to love, forgive and reconcile with one another. Although his teachings are often mistaken as idealistic, they are the most practical. He does not want people to end up in court or in prison. He wants everyone to live in peace and freedom and know the fullness of life and love....

Why do we not judge for ourselves what is right? Why do we prefer to listen to what the president and the media tell us to do? Why do we fail to form our own opinions, much less use the Gospel as a lens with which to view reality and judge between right and wrong? We are proud, angry, resentful, and hurt, refusing to reconcile with anyone, least of all our opponents? Why are we so concerned for number one?

Why do we take our chances to get ahead of others, and even risk courtroom drama and imprisonment in pursuit of money, pride, and ambition? Because judging what is right, choosing what is right, doing what is right, and reconciling with others so that we stand in the right before God is no longer our priority. We are concerned with making money, gaining power, acquiring fame, achieving success, and winning honors. We do not judge what is right, settle with opponents, and try to serve others. Instead we give away our power to do what is right and just.

In our society, where wrong is often considered right, we need a community of truth to help us know what is right and do what is right. Our local church community can encourage us to judge what is right, choose what is right, do what is right, and live right before the God of truth. As we learn to do this more and more, our faith will deepen, and we will trust God more and more. We will settle with our opponents, reconcile with everyone, and even begin to love our enemies.[2]

The command to love our enemies stands at the center of the Sermon on the Mount, Jesus' life message. Never before in history had anyone suggested such a daring proposal. Today, nearly two thousand years later, Jesus' way of love offers a way out of the world's nightmare of hatred and war. "Love for our enemies," Martin Luther King, Jr. concluded, "is the key to the solution of the problems of the world."

...our country continues to stockpile weapons of mass destruction and research new ways to kill its enemies on a massive scale. Meanwhile, some thirty-five wars are currently being waged around the world. A plague of violence tears the human family apart: nuclear incinerations on Hiroshima and Nagasaki, bombing raids, nuclear threats, executions, abortions, torture, homelessness, racism, and sexism. Our wars and weapons still have the potential to destroy all of life.

Into this overwhelming violence comes Jesus with a way out: "Love your enemies. Practice the unconditional love of God with all people as you work for justice and peace. Stop killing one another, stop waging war, stop building and maintaining nuclear weapons, and become people of nonviolence. Shower your enemies with heartfelt love. See them as your sisters and brothers, and you will win them over and learn to live at peace with one another. Then you will become like God: peacemakers."

Jesus' alternative to enmity is the persistent, reconciling love of God. He calls us to extend the all-embracing love of God across national boundaries, so that the reconciliation already created by God will be more apparent. This love will disarm all sides and bear the good fruit of peace and justice. In this great love, Jesus calls us to be God's daughters and sons and shows us how to be like God.[3]

Before Jesus blessed the peacemakers, he blessed those who hunger and thirst for justice. Then, after blessing the peacemakers, he gave his last beatitude to those persecuted for the sake of justice.[4]

Solidarity with the poor then not only keeps us grounded in the reality of poverty, injustice, and oppression; it not only helps us grow in compassion and love; it not only deepens awareness about our human dependence on God; it leads us to peace.[5]

reflection questions

1. Jesus' question "What are you looking for?" is a question to consider each day of our lives. What are you looking for at this stage of your life? Security? Comfort? Wealth? Fame? Peace? Faith?

2. How does compassion for the poor bring us closer to God?

3. Write a few words indicating what you hear Jesus calling you to seek each day for a month. Create a calendar for yourself of daily ways to live simply, nonviolently and at peace with others.

scripture to ponder

Blessed are the peacemakers, for they will be called children of God. (Matthew 5:9)

What are you looking for? (John 1:38)

And the peace of God, which surpasses all understanding, will guard your hearts and your minds in Christ Jesus. (Philippians 4:7)

concluding prayer

Dear Jesus,

Please help me to walk in your footsteps, to accompany you on your journey of love and peace, and to notice how you walk with me through my life.

Help me always to be your friend, your servant, and your companion. Give me the grace to become your disciple, that my life might reflect your life, that my story might be part of your story, that my journey might continue your journey.

Strengthen me to carry on your Gospel mission of announcing God's reign of justice and peace, denouncing injustice and war, teaching and practicing creative nonviolence, serving the poor, and taking up the cross.[6] Amen.

Notes

1 John Dear, *The Questions of Jesus: Challenging Ourselves to Discover Life's Great Answers* (New York: Image, 2004), p. 6.

2 *The Questions of Jesus,* pp. 194–195.

3 John Dear, *Jesus the Rebel: Bearer of God's Peace and Justice* (Lanham, Md.: Sheed and Ward, 2000), pp. 39–40., quoting Martin Luther King, Jr. See Martin Luther King, Jr., *Strength to Live* (Philadelphia: Fortress, 1981), 48.

4 *Living Peace,* p. 169.

5 *Living Peace,* p. 137.

6 John Dear, *Transfiguration: A Meditation on Transforming Ourselves and Our World* (New York: Image, 2007), p. 34.

Resisting Vengeance

> No testing has overtaken you that is not common to everyone.
> God is faithful, and he will not let you be tested beyond your
> strength, but with the testing he will also provide the way out so
> that you may be able to endure it.
>
> —1 Corinthians 10:13

*R*esisting vengeance is a
challenge to our gut-level tendency to strike back when we or those
we love are harmed. It's built into the fight-or-flight animal instinct
we have. Yet as spiritual creatures possessing intelligence and faith,
we are called to seek alternatives. A favorite definition of intelligence is the ability to develop alternatives. Jesus does offer us alternatives. We must make the choice to follow his alternative way of
life or to not follow him.

A Christian recently told me that her church claims that the message of the Sermon on the Mount applies only to Christ's kingdom
to come, not to the world in which we live today. She claims that
Jesus' commands to "Love your enemies" and "Do not resist evil" do

not apply to the civil state in which we live but only to the future kingdom. Therefore, governments must resist evil and strike back fiercely at enemies. That seems to mean that a Christian should learn to lead a dual life, separating political and civic life from Christian life. A Christian soldier must carry out orders to fight and kill, temporarily setting aside Christ's law to love his enemies in his heart. Is that what Jesus taught his disciples? It doesn't seem that it is. I wonder how this woman's church would interpret Jesus' command to love our enemies and put down the sword. The message that seems to override all others comes in the Lord's Prayer when we pray, "...Thy kingdom come, thy will be done on earth as it is in heaven."

The death penalty is a prime example of a vengeful act by society against one who has committed a heinous crime. Yet in killing the guilty individual, society itself takes on the role of killer. Alternatives must be applied.

The challenging questions that remain are how to reduce violent acts, how to eliminate terrorism and how to prevent anarchy while living the gospel life. Preventative maintenance is a wise approach to staying healthy, keeping our cars running and our homes in good condition. Preventative maintenance is also a way in which to prevent those of other nations and religions from viewing us as their enemies whom they should fear and attack. That's a first step in moving toward a world in which diminishing hostilities are accompanied by fewer temptations to vengeance. We must ask ourselves whether consuming vast quantities of the world's resources for nonessentials is necessary. Malnutrition and starvation plague a large percentage of the world's population while obesity is a major concern in the U.S. Excessive oil consumption accompanied by pollution has affected our land for decades, but too few find energy conservation to be a major concern. Many view conservation as an infringement on their "rights."

A close look at U.S. sanctions, military interventions and arms supply to nations in conflict sometimes finds U.S. support going to both sides. Civilian populations pay a tragic price in these civil wars. Somewhere, somehow, sometime, as we learn more about the role we play in the world, we may reach an aha moment in which we realize we need to review and revise our role as a nation.

thoughts from john

> What profit is there for one to gain the
> whole world and forfeit his life?
> —Mark 8:36; Luke 9:25; Matthew 16:26

One day in fifth-grade social studies class, we read about Martin Luther's Reformation of the church and a Counter-Reformation led by Ignatius Loyola. Ignatius had been a soldier in the Basque country of Spain, where he was severely wounded by a cannonball during battle. He spent nearly a year recovering in bed when, apparently, this question hit him like a second cannonball. His decision to take it seriously led him eventually to walk to the mountain monastery shrine of Montserrat, where he spent the night in prayer, put down his sword, and began a new life of service. Later he founded a radically new religious order of priests: the Society of Jesus, also known as the Jesuits.

Jesus' question was printed right there in black and white in my social studies textbook: "What profit is there for one to gain the whole world and forfeit his life?"

I distinctly remember looking up from my book as we read this out loud in class and turning around to see if my classmates were as shocked as I was. Could this Jesus be serious? Could this question be true? Doesn't it make the most sense?

The question stunned the saint with the funny name, we were told, but I found myself equally bowled over. What good would it be to have a great life, make a fortune, become famous and powerful, only to lose my soul and miss out on eternal life? It would not be worth it, I concluded. The point of life is not to forfeit it, to lose one's soul, and to go to hell. Rather, the point of life is to live it to the fullest here and now and forever in eternity.

Like St. Ignatius, I began to ponder the Gospel of Jesus, and I realized that the fullness of life carries certain guidelines, such as selfless love, boundless compassion, active nonviolence, relentless forgiveness, justice for the poor, and the giving of one's life for suffering humanity, like Jesus on the cross....

We all make choices about our lives: what we will do, how we will live, what goals we will pursue. In the end, we choose the kind of life we want, even if we are born in suffering and poverty. We can be selfish, resentful, violent, and mean—or we can be loving, kind, nonviolent, and compassionate.[1]

For me, then the question, "How to Stop Terrorism?" is easy. We stop terrorism first of all by stopping our own terrorism! We cannot fight terrorism by becoming terrorists. We cannot end terrorism by using the methods of terrorism to bomb and kill Iraqis, to occupy Iraq, to support the terrorist occupation of the Palestinians, and to hold the world hostage with our nuclear weapons. We must bring the troops home from Iraq, fund nonviolent democratic peacemakers in Iraq, send food and medicine to Iraq, support United Nations' nonviolent peacemaking solutions, end world hunger immediately, cut all U.S. military aid everywhere, dismantle every one of our nuclear weapons, fund jobs, education and healthcare at home and abroad, clean up the environment and teach nonviolence to everyone around the world, beginning at home in every U.S. classroom.[2]

If we take Jesus at his word and love our enemies, our lives will be disrupted. Because the world revolves around the presupposition that enemies are for hating and killing, those who cross national boundaries and political expectations will face tremendous opposition and persecution. Perhaps that is why Jesus, immediately after his command to love, commands us to pray for those who persecute us. He knows the political outcome of real enemy love. He wants us to place our persecutors at the heart of our prayer, just as our enemies are the center of our loving attention.

Perhaps we avoid this teaching because there is no easy way to love our enemies. It will not make us popular, win us friends, or advance our careers. It will not benefit anyone—except the lives of our enemies. Indeed, we may never know the results of our efforts to love our enemies, although we may have actually saved lives. We may never know the wars that have been prevented, the longstanding enmity that has been healed, or the long-term international reconciliation that began. Loving our enemies is like faith itself; it is an act of trust in God and in the future. It is an act of hope.[3]

More than half a million Iraqis, mostly children, died during the 1990s, according to UNICEF and the World Health Organization, because of these [U.S.] sanctions, which choked off the country's ability to produce clean water and dispense simple medicines. Each day, nearly two hundred children perished, their cries unheard. More than a million children under the age of five suffered chronic malnourishment....

Interviewing President Clinton's secretary of state Madeleine Albright on 60 Minutes, Leslie Stahl said: "We have heard that half a million children have died in Iraq [as a result of economic sanctions]. I mean, that is more children than died in Hiroshima. Is the price worth it?" Albright stared coldly into the camera and said, "We think the price is worth it." Her words bore that demonic line of reason, by no means unique to her—that sprang from the fire-and-brimstone days of Vietnam, the same illogic embodied in the words of a celebrated general of the time: We must destroy the village to set it free.[4]

John Dear and two Nobel Peace Laureates, Mairead Maguire of
Northern Ireland and Adolfo Pérez Esquivel of Argentina, visited Iraq
in 1999 in an attempt to "put a human face on those declared to be
inhuman—and expendable" in an attempt to stop the imposed sanctions
and the bombings in Iraq. John describes one of their experiences:

We entered Baghdad and drove directly to the Ameriyah shelter,
which the United States had bombed during the Gulf War. The first
bomb had entered the ventilation shaft at four in the morning. It
blew open the ceiling, forced the exits closed, killed seventeen people, and trapped the rest inside. Two minutes later, a second bomb
roared through the hole in the ceiling and incinerated everyone else,
some seven hundred women and children.

One woman resident of the shelter, Umm Greyda, had just
stepped outside to do the family laundry in a nearby river. One of
the only survivors, she could only watch the flames burn for hours.
Years later, she took up residence in the bombed-out shelter and
created a memorial to the victims, including her own two children
and eleven relatives.

Umm Greyda shyly welcomed us and led us through the remains
of the building. The walls of this massive concrete structure were
charred black and adorned with flowers, prayers, and hundreds of
pictures of the children who had died there. We walked through the
shelter at a solemn pace and in stunned silence. In one area, children
had been sleeping on triple-tiered bunks; the handprints of those
who were sleeping on the top were left in the melting concrete of
the ceiling. In another area was the inverse shadow of an incinerated
woman, her white silhouette against a black backdrop, her arm out-
stretched as if pointing. "I've seen this before," Adolfo said quietly,
"in Hiroshima." We came upon another inverse shadow—the out-
line of a mother holding up a child....

Next we visited the Dijla School in downtown Baghdad. When we stepped out of the van on the edge of the campus, hundreds of teenage girls approached. One emerged to welcome us. Then they began to sing, in Arabic, the great civil rights anthem, "We Shall Overcome." *Deep in my heart, we do believe, that we shall live in peace one day. We'll walk hand in hand. We are not afraid. We shall overcome someday.* After a moment, the girls rushed forward....One girl's voice rose above the others: "Why are you trying to kill us? What have we done to you?" she demanded. "We want to be friends with the kids in America!"

...[t]he girls, eyes ablaze, gave us an earful. They told us of having to scramble for cover, of their constant fear, and of the loved ones they had lost. "Your sanctions are killing our people!"[5]

reflection questions

1. What is the sacrifice indicated by John Dear's suggestion of how to stop terrorism?

2. How do you think vengeance and retaliation help or hinder the achievement of peace?

3. Reflect on ways in which God has been faithful to you.

4. Which life are you striving the hardest to attain: life here on earth or eternal life? Explain.

scripture to ponder

Father, forgive them; for they do not know what they are doing. (Luke 23:34)

For what will it profit them to gain the whole world and forfeit their life? (Mark 8:36)

Truly I tell you, just as you did it to one of the least of these who are members of my family, you did it to me. (Matthew 25:40)

...[b]e strong in the Lord and in the strength of his power. Put on the whole armor of God, so that you may be able to stand against the wiles of the devil. For our struggle is not against enemies of blood and flesh, but against the rulers, against the authorities, against the cosmic powers of this present darkness, against the spiritual forces of evil in the heavenly places. Therefore take up the whole armor of God, so that you may be able to withstand on that evil day, and having done everything, to stand firm. Stand therefore, and fasten the belt of truth around your waist, and put on the breastplate of righteousness. As shoes for your feet put on whatever will make you ready to proclaim the gospel of peace. With all of these, take the shield of faith, with which you will be able to quench all the flaming arrows of the evil one. Take the helmet of salvation, and the sword of the Spirit, which is the word of God.

Pray in the Spirit at all times in every prayer and supplication (Ephesians 6:10–18).

concluding prayer

Disarm me, God!

Come, put away the sword I still carry somewhere in my heart. Take away the violence that lingers in my soul. Make me an instrument of Your peace. You have a plan for me: fulfill it! In this world of armaments, disarm me and I shall be able to disarm others.

Come, God. There is still a trace of war and madness in my veins. Purify me, O God, and I shall let loose disarmament in the world that will cause people to praise you freely. Purify me of all violence and I shall stand before the powers and principalities without fear and free those trapped in the structures of fear and violence.

Come, God. Disarm me without my knowing it, and then, show me that you are the Disarming One, nonviolent from the beginning of time until the end of time. Disarming Presence, Unconditional Love, Great Reconciler, Suffering Servant, Patience Personified, Peaceful Mother, come, bearing peace.

Come, God. Disarm this restless heart which wanders off into apathy and selfishness, but which longs to rest in You. Lead this heart into the fire of your Love, where it can be consumed in the Flame of Nonviolence, setting fire to other hearts nearby. Let your unilateral disarmament engage me, win me over, force the scales to fall from my eyes and the weapons to be released from my hands. Push me into the violent hearts of others that I may take on their anger and release them from the chains of hatred and the bonds of violence.

Disarm me, God, and I shall disarm others. Disarm me, God, that I may be one with all humanity, all your sons and daughters. Disarm me, God, and bring me into Your reign to live forever in peace and love.[6] Amen.

Notes

1 *The Questions of Jesus,* pp. 95–96.

2 John Dear, "How to Stop Terrorism" www.fatherjohndear.org, July 2005.

3 *Jesus the Rebel,* pp. 41–42.

4 John Dear, *Persistent Peace: One Man's Struggle for a Nonviolent World* (Chicago: Loyola, 2008), pp. 311–312.

5 *Persistent Peace,* pp. 314–316.

6 *Seeds of Nonviolence,* pp. 146–147.

The Power of Gentleness

> My friends, if anyone is detected in a transgression,
> you who have received the Spirit should restore
> such a one in a spirit of gentleness.
> —Galatians 6:1

*I*n his early twenties, John Dear began to study Mahatma Gandhi's way of peace. John admired the power of Gandhi's gentle way, which led him to seek out peace and social justice for his own people, as well as for the entire world. Gandhi's gentle and persistent power changed the political and social structure of South Africa and India. He offered the world a model of active nonviolence as a way to find peaceful resolution to many differing ways of thought. Although Gandhi was a devout Hindu, he revered the way of Jesus and followed Christ's teachings in the ways of nonviolence—something that even many Christians refuse to do.

Gentleness must not be confused with weakness. Gentleness is not a wishy-washy approach to life's struggles. Rather, gentleness requires living in the deepest reality of what true power is. Gentleness demands sacrifice. Gentleness requires great courage to stand in the face of adversity without donning the world's armament of military might, revenge or personal vindication. This concept is so countercultural to a contemporary mode of thinking that "might is right" or "if someone strikes you on the cheek, slug him in the nose" that comprehending it requires much thought, prayer and contemplation.

Fear often precipitates violence. Fear, about real or imaginary issues, creeps into our minds and hearts through many sources: gossip or idle chatter, hate-mongering that stems from unfounded prejudices, exaggerated news items, misquotes in the media, or failure to view life from the perspective of another person, nation or culture. Fear can be spawned by superficial views of those who are "different." Many find it difficult to accept those with a different skin color, gender, sexual orientation, political stance, nationality, age or even mode of dress.

When fear creeps in, our animal instincts of fight or flight stir within us. But we are not just animals. We are thinking, spiritual creatures. As rational and spiritual human beings, we have other options. We can evaluate what we hear before reacting. This enables us to act in wise ways to what seems to threaten our lives as we know them. As Christians we can evaluate what causes us to fear in the light of the gospel message of Jesus. As we filter events through Jesus' message of love and forgiveness, we can develop alternatives to fighting or fleeing, certainly to hating. On our way to loving our enemies as Jesus teaches, we can begin by respecting the otherness of the other.

I believe Gandhi was right. Living out his vow of nonviolence, Gandhi declared, "I am prepared to die but there is no cause for which I am prepared to kill."

The words of Martin Luther King, Jr., hold true for us all: "The choice before us is not violence and nonviolence. It is nonviolence or nonexistence." We need to learn the ways of Jesus, to love our ene-mies, to seek justice for the poor, to speak the truth of peace, to put down our swords, to beat our nuclear weapons into plowshares of peace, and to become sons and daughters of God, brothers and sisters of each other. We need to commit ourselves anew to the way, the truth, and the life of nonviolence....

The journey of nonviolence, I am discovering, is an inner journey into the spiritual depths of nonviolence, into God. If I am open enough to the God who disarms my heart every day, my life, like the lives of all peacemakers, can become a nonviolent, spiritual explosion. My life can participate in God's transformation of the world into a realm of justice and peace.[1]

The day before India's leader Mahatma Gandhi was assassinated, a reporter asked him for advice. "Have nothing to do with power," Gandhi replied. After a lifetime in the public eye as the hero of polit-ical liberation, Gandhi learned from Jesus to run in the opposite direc-tion of the world, to renounce the world's power, to seek powerless-ness. Try not to win success, reach the top of the heap, or dominate others, Gandhi recommended. Instead, discover the fullness of life at the bottom of the heap. Protect your soul. Stand with the powerless and discover the power of powerlessness, like Jesus on the cross.[2]

We were not created to live in fear. Rather, we were created to live in peace and love with ourselves, with one another, with the whole human race, and with God. If we believe in God, look for God, listen for God, listen to Jesus, and stay centered in Jesus' presence, we will no longer be terrified. We will not have time or energy to be afraid because we will be so focused on Jesus. This will not happen overnight, however, and it will not come easily. There is no quick ride to fearlessness. It is a lifetime journey that requires discipline, community, prayer, simplified lifestyle, selfless love, and a compassionate heart toward one's self and humanity. Over time, the Scriptures and the saints promise, we can grow into fearlessness.[3]

Gandhi was, first and foremost, a religious man in search of God. For more than fifty years, he pursued truth, proclaiming that the best way to discover truth is through the practice of active, faith-based nonviolence.[4]

"I did not move a muscle when I first heard that the atom bomb had wiped out Hiroshima," Gandhi told an interviewer. "On the contrary, I said to myself, 'Unless now the world adopts nonviolence, it will spell certain suicide for humanity.' Nonviolence is the only thing the atom bomb cannot destroy."[5]

"Today, the United States maintains thousands of nuclear weapons with no international movement toward disarmament....

"The country that adopts a policy of total disarmament, without waiting for its neighbors, will be able to lead the world away from hatred, fear, and mistrust toward the true community, the harmony of all people."[6]

"Satyagrahis[7] must never forget the distinction between evil and the evildoer," [Gandhi wrote]. "They must not harbor ill will or bitterness against the evildoer. They may not even employ needlessly offensive language against evildoing persons, however unrelieved their evil might be."[8]

In the months after the September 11, 2001, attacks, many felt despair not only because of the horrific terrorism but because of the U.S. retaliatory response in the bombing of Afghanistan and Iraq. During those initial dark months, some family members who lost loved ones in the 9/11 attacks joined together to speak out against war and urge peaceful resolutions. They formed September Eleventh Families for Peaceful Tomorrows, a nonprofit, antiwar group in memory of their deceased loved ones. Their first public action was a 250-mile walk from New York's Ground Zero to the ruins of the Pentagon. Then they sent a delegation to Afghanistan to listen to the Afghani families who lost loved ones during the U.S. bombing raids. Instead of giving in to despair and discouragement, they became signs of light and hope and encouraged others to confront U.S. retaliatory war-making, to end our own terrorist attacks, and to create a more nonviolent world.

If we look closely, we can see signs of God's light breaking through our darkness and despair, giving us hope and encouragement, sending us forth to complete the work of justice and disarmament. One day, when the people of the United States finally wake up; dismantle their nuclear weapons; spend their billions of dollars to eradicate hunger, disease, homelessness, illiteracy, and unemployment; clean up the oceans and the earth; and renounce war forever, humanity itself will be transfigured and the light of Christ will shine brightly and lead us to an astonishing breakthrough of global hope and encouragement. Humanity will catch a glimpse of the nonviolent reign of God and set to work preparing to welcome its full arrival.[9]

reflection questions

1. What is truth?
2. What do you believe is the best way to discover truth? How do you employ that way in your own life?
3. What people, nation or culture do you need to view through God's eyes rather than personal prejudices? How can you begin to accomplish this new view?

scripture to ponder

By the tender mercy of our God,
the dawn from on high will break upon us,
to give light to those who sit in darkness and in the shadow of death,
to guide our feet into the way of peace. (Luke 1:78–79)

I therefore, the prisoner in the Lord, beg you to lead a life worthy of the calling to which you have been called, with all humility and gentleness, with patience, bearing with one another in love, making every effort to maintain the unity of the Spirit in the bond of peace. (Ephesians 4:1–3)

As God's chosen ones, holy and beloved, clothe yourselves with compassion, kindness, humility, meekness, and patience. Bear with one another and, if anyone has a complaint against another, forgive each other; just as the Lord has forgiven you, so you also must forgive. Above all, clothe yourselves with love, which binds everything together in perfect harmony. And let the peace of Christ rule in your hearts, to which indeed you were called in the one body. And be thankful. (Colossians 3:12–15)

...[p]ursue righteousness, godliness, faith, love, endurance, gentleness. (1 Timothy 6:11)

"Go out and stand on the mountain before the LORD, for the LORD is about to pass by," Now there was a great wind, so strong that it was splitting mountains and breaking rocks in pieces before the LORD, but the LORD was not in the wind; and after the wind an earthquake, but the LORD was not in the earthquake; and after the earthquake a fire, but the LORD was not in the fire; and after the fire a sound of sheer silence. When Elijah heard it, he wrapped his face in his mantle and went and stood at the entrance of the cave. Then there came a voice to him that said, "What are you doing here, Elijah?" (1 Kings 19:11–13)

c o n c l u d i n g   p r a y e r

The following is a prayer meditation on Elijah's experience of the sheer silence, which in some translations is described as a gentle breeze.

MAKE ME A GENTLE BREEZE
(A reflection on 1 Kings 19:9–12)

Lord, make me a gentle breeze.
Let me stroke the heads of little ones.
Send me across the gnarled faces of the old.

Lord, make me a gentle breeze.
Allow me to dry the tears on the cheeks of the bereft.
Let me skip over the teardrops
    on cheeks of those whose cups run over with joy.

Lord, make me a gentle breeze.
Let me move among your people
    caress them, hold them, love them.

Lord, make me a gentle breeze.
May I stir the spiritual waters of those who are still.
Keep me gentle lest I overwhelm the still more gentle.

Lord, make me a gentle breeze.
Let me rest assured

in the Source of my strength lest I become a wind.

Lord, make me a gentle breeze.
Use my passing to bear your Spirit where you will
    to lift hopes, scatter doubts and bear despair away.

Lord, make me a gentle breeze.
Give me a prayer to whisper as I flow.
Let me murmur praise for everything.

Lord, make me a gentle breeze.[10]

God, I beg You: give us your peace. Grant us your spirit that we may all repent from the ways of violence and convert to your Way of Nonviolence.[11]

Notes
1 John Dear, *Disarming the Heart: Toward a Vow of Nonviolence* (Scottsdale, Pa.: Herald, 1993), pp. 26–27.
2 *The Questions of Jesus*, p. 97.
3 *Transfiguration*, pp. 150–151.
4 *Mohandas Gandhi: Essential Writings*, John Dear, ed. (Maryknoll, N.Y.: Orbis, 2002), p. 17.
5 *Mohandas Gandhi: Essential Writings*, p. 143.
6 *Mohandas Gandhi: Essential Writings*, p. 144.
7 *Satyagrahis* is a term to describe those who follow Gandhi's passive resistance to violence. The name comes from the Sanskrit words *satya*, which means "truth," and *agraha*, which means "persistence."
8 *Mohandas Gandhi: Essential Writings*, pp. 90–91.
9 *Transfiguration*, pp. 223–224.
10 Patricia Normile, *Prayers for Care Givers* (Cincinnati: St. Anthony Messenger Press, 1995), pp. 96–97.
11 *Seeds of Nonviolence*, p. 148.

Mary, Queen of Peace

> And blessed is she who believed that there
> would be a fulfillment of what was
> spoken to her by the Lord.
> —Luke 1:45

*W*hy has Mary been granted the title "Queen of Peace?" A simple answer is that she is the Mother of the Prince of Peace. This is certainly true. But Mary, through her own choices, faithfulness and willingness to submit to God's will, merits the title "Queen of Peace" in her own right as well. Mary was a radical woman who was willing to submit to God's will in spite of the possibility of being stoned to death for her choice. She is the perfect example of what a young, poor and powerless woman can initiate in the world by saying a resounding yes to God. Most of us possess considerably more clout in our communities than Mary had in hers. A vibrant, intelligent young woman told me how it felt to live in her native land in South America under a dictatorship. "I had no voice. Nothing wrong could be addressed," she said. Mary's circumstances as a woman in first-century Palestine would have been similar.

We in the U.S. have the right to vote for our leadership. We can vocalize our convictions about what is right and wrong according to the gospel values that we profess to embody. Yes, sometimes there are repercussions, like possibly being outcast by our peers for our beliefs. Yet freedom of speech and freedom of the press allow us to write letters to the editors of our local publications, to speak out for peace at public gatherings—no, not hostile messages, but wise messages that encourage others to act as Mary did. Like Mary, we are to seek truth, speak with love and act with faith in God and conviction that we are following God's directives in our lives.

Whether we are women or men, Mary offers us a model of how to approach God's call to action for peace in our lives. We listen to God through varied sources: the Scriptures, trusted spiritual guides, our own prayers. Then we discern what wise and courageous actions we are to take. And we move forward—toward peace—with confidence and hope.

thoughts from john

The story of Mary's encounter with the angel and her visitation to her cousin Elizabeth is all too familiar, but two words in the text shake us into realizing how urgent her love was. We are told that Mary set out "with haste." The journey on foot to Elizabeth's home, if she lived in Ein Karim as tradition holds, would have been a dangerous ninety-mile pilgrimage from Nazareth through mountains, desert, woods, soldiers, and robbers. She sets off quickly, like Israel in exile, a scene the entire Holy Family will reprise in their flight from Herod into Egypt. Mary puts her fears and worries aside to be with her cousin, to assist in her delivery, and to share their amazing experiences with God's angel. Mary does not wait; she takes action immediately. She is a doer.[1]

In these classic Christian stories of the Annunciation, the Visitation, and the Magnificat, I discovered three basic movements of the spiritual life, from contemplative nonviolence to active nonviolence to prophetic nonviolence. In Mary's journey, we see the basic steps on the road to peace. When taken as a whole, the Annunciation, the Visitation, and the Magnificat (Luke 1:26–55) show how Mary became a peacemaker to our world. Through her contemplative nonviolence she welcomed the God of peace into her life and the world. Through her active nonviolence she reached out to a person in need and loved her neighbor. Through her prophetic nonviolence she publicly announced God's reign of justice for the poor and God's mercy at work throughout history. Through her example, Mary teaches us how to be peacemakers by becoming people of contemplative nonviolence who practice active, and ultimately prophetic, nonviolence.

The Gospel of Luke leads one to assume that Jesus learned nonviolence from his mother. Just as Mary taught Jesus to worship the God of peace, to be at peace with everyone, and to proclaim God's reign of peace to a war-making world, Mary calls us to become people of peace.[2]

Mary is not a passive saint. A contemplative and an activist, a mystic and a revolutionary, Mary is the mother of God and so she boldly proclaims God's word of nonviolence to the world of violence, God's revolution of justice to the world of injustice. She is blatantly political. She does not just rock the boat or shake up the status quo. She turns over the tables of the culture. Mary is dangerous. She disturbs the culture's complacency and stirs up trouble. From the perspective of the rebellious Mary of Nazareth, everything from this point onward is different. Everything is called into question. Everything must change. Yes, she is full of grace, light, love, mercy, and kindness. And she is trouble for every empire, every proponent of violence, every war-maker, every millionaire, every advocate of systemic injustice.

In Mary's day, people were routinely arrested and brutally executed for saying the things Mary declared to Elizabeth. Mary's message is radical revolution, pure and simple: God has thrown down the rulers from their thrones. God has lifted up the lowly. God has filled the hungry with good things. God has sent the rich away empty.

Such serious words cause trouble in our own times, too. Mary's Magnificat was banned in Argentina in the mid-1970s because the Mothers of the Disappeared published it as a call for nonviolent resistance to the military junta. The words are so powerful, they are considered by some to be dangerous.

Mary speaks about political, economic, and social conversion, about nonviolent revolution. She points out God's preferential option for the poor, God's opposition to injustice, and God's faithful commitment to nonviolence and to the community of nonviolence.[3]

Though the times are deeply disturbing, there are signs of hope. As I write, on January 24, 2002, the Pope has gathered over two hundred leaders representing the world's major religions in Assisi, home of St. Francis, for a day of prayer for peace. Surrounded by imams, rabbis, patriarchs, nuns, and monks, John Paul II stood in front of the Basilica of St. Francis and urged religious people everywhere to repudiate violence, especially in light of the September 11th attacks.

We must fend off "the dark clouds of terrorism, hatred, armed conflict, which in these last few months have grown particularly ominous on humanity's horizon," the Pope began. "Whoever uses religion to foment violence contradicts religion's deepest and truest inspiration," he said. It is "essential" that religious people "in the clearest and most radical way repudiate violence," he continued, "all violence, starting with the violence that seeks to clothe itself in religion. There is no religious goal which can possibly justify the use of violence by people against people," he concluded.

Such a gathering has only occurred on two other occasions in history, in 1986, in a day of prayer for nuclear disarmament, and in 1993, in a prayer for an end to the Balkans war. Such gatherings offer a hopeful sign of God's mercy working in our time, leading us to a new age of interfaith dialogue, cooperation, nonviolent alternatives to war, and the prophetic call for peace and justice.

Likewise, Mary's proclamation of hope challenges our despair. Her Magnificat directs us to look hard at our lives and our world for the presence of God. Do we see the God at work in history's nonviolent movements against injustice? Do we recognize God's mercy and nonviolence at work today among ordinary people of faith and conscience who struggle against poverty, oppression, injustice, war, terrorism, imperialism, consumerism, and nuclear weapons? Do we believe that God is a God of peace, a God of compassion, a God of justice? Dare we join God's movement of nonviolent transformation, the abolition of war, nuclear weapons, and injustice, once and for all?

Mary invites us to take a leap of faith, like her, to say Yes to God, to trust in God's holiness and mercy, and to recognize God's mercy and nonviolent action at work in our hearts and in our world. The Magnificat calls us to become like Mary, like God, holy, merciful, and nonviolent. Then we too will know better what the holiness of God means, and how God's mercy is at work today healing and reconciling us all.[4]

Mary is no longer afraid. She runs out into the world with a heart full of love. She has become God's peacemaker.[5]

The history of war has proved that violence is not just immoral and illegal, but downright impractical. It simply does not work. It cannot solve our problems. It only foments further problems down the road. It leaves a trail of blood, bodies, tears, and resentment. Violence in response to violence can only lead to further violence.

The great lesson of the twentieth century is that war has not resolved our problems and brought us peace. It has only led to greater militarism and more war. This destructive behavior cannot go on forever. At some point, the world will break. This is our future if our present course continues.[6]

reflection questions

John offers us the following reflection questions that pour from his heart and mind. Try to spend a few moments trying to respond to them as best as you can:

Do I wait upon God day after day? Can I live as a humble slave of God, trying to do only God's will and not my own selfish will? Dare I let go of my false self? Do I want to see God? Would I truly want to join God's salvific work? Can I accept the life of holy obedience to God and live in the freedom of God's grace? Will I become the person God intended me to be: God's loving, compassionate, peacemaking son [daughter]? Dare I choose to be chosen by God? Can I ever say with Mary, "I am the servant of the God of peace, let God's will for me be done?"[7]

scripture to ponder

...My soul magnifies the Lord,
   and my spirit rejoices in God my Savior,
for he has looked with favor on the lowliness of his servant.
   Surely, from now on all generations will call me blessed;
for the Mighty One has done great things for me,
   and holy is his name.
His mercy is for those who fear him

from generation to generation.
He has shown strength with his arm;
   he has scattered the proud in the thoughts of their hearts.
He has brought down the powerful from their thrones,
   and lifted up the lowly;
he has filled the hungry with good things,
   and sent the rich away empty.
He has helped his servant Israel,
   in remembrance of his mercy,
according to the promise he made to our ancestors,
   to Abraham and to his descendants forever. (Luke 1:46–55)

c o n c l u d i n g   p r a y e r

MOTHER TERESA'S PRAYER TO MARY

Mary, be my mother now.[8]

Notes

1 John Dear, *Mary of Nazareth: Prophet of Peace* (Notre Dame, Ind.: Ave Maria, 2003), pp. 60–61.

2 *Mary of Nazareth*, pp. 20–21.

3 *Mary of Nazareth*, pp. 88–89.

4 *Mary of Nazareth*, pp. 102–104.

5 *Mary of Nazareth*, p. 55.

6 *Mary of Nazareth*, p. 14.

7 *Mary of Nazareth*, p. 47.

8 *Mary of Nazareth*, p. 127. (In the early 1990s, John Dear was asked to arrange phone conversations for Mother Teresa as she appealed to various governors and judges on behalf of those condemned to death row. Two or three times she asked John to recommend one of her favorite prayers to those on death row. Mother Teresa told John this: "Tell them to pray to Mary with great confidence, saying 'Mary, be my mother now.' ")

Overcoming Outrage

> ...your anger does not produce God's righteousness.
>
> —James 1:20

*O*utrage engulfs our culture: road rage, domestic rage, sports rage, government rage, even self rage. Outrage in itself is not evil or even wrong. Often it is quite justified. A child is murdered or abused. A poor widow trying to fix up her home is cheated of what little she has by an unscrupulous contractor. An elderly couple is robbed and left tied up in their home. A drive-by shooting leaves an innocent bystander paralyzed for life. Animals are neglected or tortured. Nations attack nations. Civil wars ravage the people and their lands. Rage fills us because of the injustice of the acts. What we do with our outrage is the significant factor.

One persistent contributing factor to instances of minor rage is a cultural and personal need to have things our own way. Someone unintentionally cuts us off in traffic and our internal uproar surpasses a reasonable point. At an athletic event, I recently witnessed such an episode. Parking lot traffic leaving the event was gently and peacefully merging into an exit line when the driver of one car thought another driver had endangered his vehicle. He leaped from his very pricey car, screaming and raging, and began pounding on the window of the other car, threatening the driver even though his car was unscathed, not even threatened with a scrape. Other drivers who had clearly seen that no wrong had occurred emerged from their cars. One person calmly suggested that the raging bull return to his car. Peace was restored by a calming word applied to the violent verbal assault that had taken place. Undoubtedly, a few hearts were pounding faster but peace was restored and the slow-moving traffic slogged on.

Even though one may not intend to harm another with words, an inadvertent comment may still cause another to fume. A starting point in dealing with such minor offenses is first of all to acknowledge the other person's feelings. As individuals, we all have a right to feel and think differently and approach matters differently. Allowing such incidents to pass frees us from the pent-up anger and internal hostility that creates a breeding ground for the further growth of rage. Forgiving and moving on is often the best approach. Initially, a gut-level response may be to strike out at one who has offended us. A violent response to a violent act only precipitates more violence. A brief saying speaks to such moments: "I'd rather be right than have my own way." Being right involves applying prudent, correct behavior to a potentially explosive situation in spite of what another person may have done. Put in simple terms, two wrongs do not make a right. The age-old advice to stop and count to ten has merit. We might even say a silent prayer, like the Lord's Prayer, or a blessing for the offender. Our peace of mind will be stabilized and transfer to the one with whom conflict arises. Our ability to deal reasonably and peacefully with the situation will be enhanced.

When offenses are more grave in nature, dealing with the issue in constructive ways is always more beneficial than physical or verbal expressions of outrage. Justice precedes peace. Therefore, finding ways to bring about just resolutions to unjust situations lays the groundwork for peace in communities and within us. A community work group might help a victimized elderly individual with home upkeep. Volunteering at an animal shelter may foster care for unwanted animals. Vigils honoring those who have suffered may not change what has happened but they do offer spiritual and emotional support to victims who are bereft and bereaved. When put into action, communal support can say, "Never again! Never will our community allow such outrageous behavior." Turning the other cheek is an alternative to rage, as long as the turning of the cheek points to a new direction in order to create nonviolent actions, and is not simply a passive ignoring of wrongdoing.

Being aware of people and situations that surround us is one way to intervene before something outrageous happens. A child or an adult who is sullen or lonely, without visible family affection or nurturing relationships, may need intervention. Rage is frequently spawned when individuals feel excluded and without worth. A listening ear can forestall or defuse feelings of rage.

If we are honest, we might acknowledge that cases of outrage occur when our ego is insulted. This may be painful to accept, but growth producing when we determine to deal with its reality. When we feel angry, we may ask ourselves whether our rage has been validly roused against an incident of injustice or whether our self-image has been affronted by the situation. When we discover that the injury to self is at the heart of our anger, we can bring that injured self to the Lord for healing. If our anger is rooted in injustice in the world, we can commence searching for ways in which to remedy the injustice. As individuals or small groups we may not possess the influence to effect change that will remove all the injustices in the world, but through the decision to change and opt out of rage, we will have removed anger from one place in the world—ourselves.

Prayer is a way to overcome outrage. Prayer calms our spirits, engages our wills and leads us to active ways to implement nonviolence and work toward justice in the world.

thoughts from john

We do not want to forget that we are God's children, but we do forget, each one of us. Nonviolence is a way of remembering and recalling, every day of our lives, who we are and what we are about—and returning to that truth of life whenever we forget.[1]

Pursuing peace at every level of life—beginning within our own hearts and souls, and reaching out toward every human being alive on the planet—is the greatest and most fulfilling challenge one can undertake with one's life. But making peace in a world at war is an act greater than any of us. It is a spiritual journey that begins in the heart and takes us on a road not of our own choosing. But because it is a spiritual journey, a course charted by the God of peace, it is filled with the simplest but greatest of blessings.[2]

Nonviolence is the peace of heart in which we love ourselves, our neighbors, all humanity, and God. It is the act of making peace, resisting death, and choosing life. It means living out of a disarmed heart.[3]

[November 16, 1989] At around nine o'clock in the morning, I was in my room at my desk when someone knocked on the door. Steve Kelly walked in looking stricken. Had I heard the news? he asked, then began to cry. Only a few hours earlier, around one o'clock, twenty-eight soldiers of the Salvadoran army, nineteen of them trained at the School of the Americas, had raided the University of Central America in El Salvador, seized the sleeping Jesuits in the community there, dragged them outside, and shot them dead. Ignacio Ellacuría, Segundo Montes, Ignacio Martín-Baró, Joaquín López y López, Amando

López, and Juan Ramón Moreno. Murdered along with them were Julia Elba Ramos and Celina Ramos, a mother and daughter who worked at a nearby Jesuit community and had come to take shelter at the university.

Later in the morning, the Jesuits' bodies were found lying on the lawn. Their brains had been removed and laid beside them, a macabre sign and an implicit threat: Some things we will not permit you to ponder. This is what you get if you *think* about war and peace. (Father Jon Sobrino, who also lived in the community, would have been killed as well had he not been speaking at a conference in Bangkok.)

My heart stopped. The ground beneath me gave way, but this was an earthquake of a different order. Great men I had known and admired had been murdered by soldiers trained by the United States—and some within our borders, as the world would later learn. . . .

We had turned a corner. Shortly after, Congress cut military aid to El Salvador, and in 1992 a peace accord was signed. The bombing of villages was put to a stop. The Jesuits, the four churchwomen, the countless martyrs, dear Romero—they had not died in vain.[4]

As we accept God's disarming love every day we become more and more who we already are   beloved sons and daughters of God. In this disarming practice of remembrance, we live our lives in the Spirit of God, growing more and more aware at each moment of God's active presence in us, in the human family, in the whole world.

Once we remember who we are, we realize we could never hurt— much less kill—another person. We could never wage war, sit idly by while millions starve to death, or share in the systemic violence that leads to poverty and the arms race. This constant remembrance of the unity of all life calls us to renounce violence, no matter how noble the cause.[5]

...[O]ur country continues to stockpile weapons of mass destruction and research new ways to kill its enemies on a massive scale. Meanwhile, some thirty-five wars are currently being waged around the world.... A plague of violence tears the human family apart: nuclear incinerations on Hiroshima and Nagasaki, bombing raids, nuclear threats, executions, abortions, torture, homelessness, racism, and sexism. Our wars and weapons still have the potential to destroy all of life.

Into this overwhelming violence comes Jesus with a way out: "Love your enemies. Practice the unconditional love of God with all people as you work for justice and peace. Stop killing one another, stop waging war, stop building and maintaining nuclear weapons, and become people of nonviolence. Shower your enemies with heartfelt love. See them as your sisters and brothers, and you will win them over and learn to live at peace with one another. Then you will become like God: peacemakers."

Jesus' alternative to enmity is the persistent, reconciling love of God. He calls us to extend the all-embracing love of God across national boundaries, so that the reconciliation already created by God will be more apparent. This love will disarm all sides and bear the good fruit of peace and justice. In this great love, Jesus calls us to be God's daughters and sons and shows us how to be like God.[6]

"Mute prayer is my greatest weapon," Mohandas Gandhi once wrote. I long to be a person of prayer, a mystic, a person who seeks God. I long to go to a quiet mountain place to pray (Lk 6:12).... But I find prayer is a struggle. It requires release of my false self and coming before God as I really am, with my many flaws and concerns and... the basic plea, "Lord, I believe. Help my unbelief" (Mk 9:24). I know I cannot remain faithful or even survive as a Christian without this struggle. Prayer fortifies my life.[7]

I meditate on the turbulent life of Jesus—hated by the world, rejected by friends, hunted by authorities, used by many, abused by others. I embrace the Lord and feel a calming spirit come upon me. This deep peace heals me, draws me out, and transcends my [prison] cell. For a few minutes, I know the peace I have been seeking.[8]

The good spirit of God wants us first and always to be at peace if we are going to seek peace, speak peace and promote peace with justice in God's name. All the way to peace is peace filled, the ancients said. "While you are proclaiming peace with your lips, be careful to have it even more fully in your heart," St. Francis wrote long ago.[9]

reflection questions

1. How has outrage, your own or that of others, helped you? How has it harmed you?
2. What alternatives to outrage could have been employed in this situation?
3. Who is your God? A warlike, angry, punishing, violent God? Or a God of unconditional love who forgives us and leads us on the path to peace? How does your view of God affect your reactions in outrageous situations?
4. Consider the thought: Violence begets violence begets violence begets violence....

scripture to ponder

So make up your minds not to prepare your defense in advance.... By your endurance you will gain your souls (Luke 21:14, 19).

[W]hat does the LORD require of you
but to do justice, and to love kindness,
and to walk humbly with your God? (Micah 6:8)

Do not resist an evildoer. But if anyone strikes you on the right cheek, turn the other also; and if anyone wants to sue you and take your coat, give your cloak as well; and if anyone forces you to go one mile, go also the second mile. Give to everyone who begs from you, and do not refuse anyone who wants to borrow from you. (Matthew 5:39–42)

You have heard that it was said, "You shall love your neighbor and hate your enemy." But I say to you, Love your enemies and pray for those who persecute you, so that you may be children of your Father in heaven.... Be perfect, therefore, as your heavenly Father is perfect. (Matthew 5:43–45, 48)

concluding prayer

PRAYER FOR A DISARMED HEART

God of nonviolence,
thank you for your love and your gift of peace.
Give me the grace and the courage
    to live a life of nonviolence
so that I may be faithful to Jesus our peacemaker.
Send your Spirit of nonviolence
    that I may love everyone
as my sister and my brother and not fear or hurt anyone.
Help me to be an instrument of you peace;
to struggle for justice and work to end war;
to respond with love and not to retaliate with violence;
to accept suffering in the struggle for justice
and never to inflict suffering or death on others;
to live more simply and to accompany the poor;
to resist systemic violence and death;
to choose life for all your children.
Guide me along the way of nonviolence.
Help me to speak the truth of peace,
    to practice compassion,

to act justly and to walk with you

in a contemplative spirit of nonviolent love.

Disarm my heart

and I shall be your instrument

to disarm other hearts.

Lead me, God of nonviolence,

   with the whole human family

into your nonviolent reign of justice and peace

where there is no fear, no war, no injustice,

   and no violence.

I ask this in the name of Jesus, the Way of nonviolence.[10]

Amen.

Notes

1 *Disarming the Heart*, p. 11.

2 *Living Peace*, pp. 16–17.

3 *Disarming the Heart*, p. 44.

4 *A Persistent Peace*, pp. 186–187, 195.

5 *Disarming the Heart*, p. 45.

6 *Jesus the Rebel*, pp. 39–40.

7 John Dear, *Peace Behind Bars: A Peacemaking Priest's Journal from Jail*, (Franklin, Wis.: Sheed and Ward, 1999), p. 173.

8 *Peace Behind Bars*, p. 190.

9 *Seeds of Nonviolence*, p. 335.

10 *Disarming the Heart*, p. 174.

Facing Evil With Love

> Do not be afraid...
> –Matthew 28:10

*fter taking a shortcut, I* ended up walking through a tough part of our city. I probably should not have ventured there alone—a seemingly hopeless part of town—with its boarded up buildings, homeless folks sleeping in doorways or drinking the afternoon away from bottles shrouded in brown paper bags. I stepped up my pace as I saw a young man approach me. He looked quite threatening. I was probably judging him by his clothing, which featured a long gold chain dangling from his pocket, pants rolled up to the knee on one leg, two mismatched shoes and two different socks, and a very unusual hat. "Make no eye contact," I advised myself as I jogged toward him. Just then my toe struck a sizable stone that I had not seen on the sidewalk. The stone launched directly into his bare shin! He winced in pain. What did I do? I dashed up to the formerly threatening guy, grasped him by the shoulders, almost hugging him, and asked, "Are you OK?" I

found myself looking into kind eyes. He assured me he was OK. We smiled and went our ways. I've never forgotten how I had feared evil and met forgiveness and kindness.

I had faced an imaginary evil. Yet we know that true evil does exist in our world. How do we face intrinsic malevolence? My inclination had been to avoid looking in the eye of what I perceived to be evil. In reality, avoiding evil may be a way of pretending it doesn't exist. To be overcome, evil must be looked in the eye but looked at with love—our love, the love of the Lord. That does not mean acceptance of what is wrong or evil. It simply means to wash the evil one and evil acts with the love that passes all understanding.

An angry, violent man was holding an elderly couple hostage in their home. The woman saw beyond the evil intent threatening her to the troubled human behind it. She offered to prepare a meal for him since he appeared to be hungry. He accepted. As she cooked and as he ate, they talked. All the while his gun lay on the table. He told her about his life's problems and his overwhelming anger. She told him about her life and her God. Ultimately, the intruder agreed to surrender to authorities. No one was harmed. One man was greatly helped because someone looked evil directly in the eye and offered comfort and understanding that expressed God's love.

One legend I love is about the people of Denmark and how they faced the evil of the Holocaust. The story tells that many non-Jewish Danes wore the yellow star of David in solidarity with Jews who, under Nazi edict, had to identify themselves with this emblem. Myth often reveals a deeper truth. These stories remind us that the greatest factor in preventing us from facing evil with love is fear. Yet Jesus repeatedly tells us in the Scriptures, "Do not be afraid." Still we fear. We fear pain. We fear loss. We fear death. Each fear cries out to be healed by God's overriding love.

AN INTRODUCTION TO HIS LIFE AND WORK

Where there is hatred, let me sow love—
Transform the hatred in my own heart into your love, understanding, compassion, forgiveness, and grace. Disarm me so that hatred disappears and love flows freely to all. Use me to build bridges between divided peoples, to soothe their fears, to see one another as sisters and brothers. Let me sow the seeds of love that will bear fruit in a new spirit of repentance, mercy, disarmament, justice, and liberation for the poor. Extinguish the flames of war and spring forth your life-giving waters of love—in the church, between the races and the genders, the rich and the poor, the old and the young, in Baghdad and Washington, D.C., in Calcutta and Mississippi, in Rwanda and East Timor, in Haiti and El Salvador, in South Africa and the Philippines, between East and West, North and South. Help me to sow seeds of agape, compassion, and peace, and to water and care for those seeds that they may flower into your reign of nonviolence.[1]

I live in a tiny, remote, impoverished, three block long town in the desert of northeastern New Mexico. Everyone in town—and the whole state—knows that I am against the occupation of Iraq, that I have called for the closing of Los Alamos, and that as a priest, I have been preaching, like the Pope, against the bombing of Baghdad.

Last week, it was announced that the local National Guard unit..., based in the nearby Armory, was being deployed to Iraq.... I was not surprised when yellow ribbons immediately sprang up....But I was surprised the following morning to hear 75 soldiers singing, shouting and screaming as they jogged down Main Street, passed our St. Joseph's church, back and forth around town for an hour. It was

6 a.m., and they woke me up with their war slogans, chants like "Kill! Kill! Kill!" and "Swing your guns from left to right; we can kill those guys all night."

Their chants were disturbing, but this is war. They have to psyche themselves up for the kill. They have to believe that flying off to some tiny, remote desert town in Iraq where they will march in front of someone's house and kill poor young Iraqis has some greater meaning besides cold-blooded murder.... I have been to Iraq, and led a delegation of Nobel Peace Prize winners to Baghdad in 1999, and I know that the people there are no different than the people here.

The screaming and chanting went on...it was quite scary because the desert is normally a place of perfect peace and silence.

Suddenly, at 7 a.m., the shouting got dramatically louder. I looked out the front window of the house where I live, next door to the church, and there they were—all 75 of them, standing yards away from my front door, in the street right in front of my house and our church, shouting and screaming at the top of their lungs, "Kill! Kill! Kill!" Their commanders had planted them there and were egging them on.

I was astonished and appalled. I suddenly realized that I do not need to go to Iraq; the war had come to my front door.... I decided I had to do something.... I...walked out the front door right into the middle of the street. They stopped shouting and looked at me, so I said loudly...for all to hear, "In the name of God, I order all of you to stop this nonsense, and not to go to Iraq. I want all of you to quit the military, disobey your orders to kill, and not to kill anyone. I do not want you to get killed. I want you to practice the love and nonviolence of Jesus. God does not bless war.... God does not support war. Stop all this and go home. God bless you."

Their jaws dropped, their eyeballs popped and they stood in shock and silence, looking steadily at me. Then they burst out laughing. Finally, the commander dismissed them and they left....

In the end, the episode for me was an experience of hope. We must be making a difference if the soldiers have to march at our front doors. That they failed to convert me or intimidate me, that they had to listen to my side of the story, may haunt their consciences as they travel to Iraq. No matter what happens, they have heard loud and clear the good news that God does not want them to kill anyone. I hope we can all learn the lesson.[2]

The Gospel proclaims...Love your enemies! Do not kill them. Do not threaten to kill them. Do not pay for killing them. Do not obey orders to kill them. Do not obey the laws which legalize their killing. Do not kill them because you need the job. Do not kill them because you want to "be all that you can be." Do not be complicit in killing. Do not hoard property or possessions because the government may use them as its excuse to kill. Do not look the other way while 40 wars are waged, while millions starve to death and while preparations for nuclear war continue presently, quietly, in your name.

For God there are no enemies. God sees no borders and no differences. God sees only love. God is not a god of war; nor a god of violence; nor a god of deterrence; nor an unjust, wrathful god, eagerly waiting to destroy us. God loves us all and wants us to love one another. The first step towards loving our enemies is dismantling our weapons. We cannot rationally claim to love our enemies while we prepare to kill them. If we are going to obey God's command to love our enemies, we will have to risk disarmament. We ourselves will have to confront these weapons. The government will never disarm because it does not obey God. As followers of Jesus, we must begin anew this process of disarmament by beating our nuclear swords into plowshares of peace.

Until we disarm, we mock God. Our weapons are aimed at God's heart. These weapons of destruction may destroy other human beings who our government labels as enemies, but our willingness to use them destroys our souls.

As we disarm and love our enemies, we fulfill God's command. Perhaps then the question before us is: How much do we love God? How seriously do we take God? Will we obey God's command?[3]

Our hearts are to be pure in all things, so that the nonviolence we practice in the world reflects the nonviolent spirit in our hearts. "You have heard that it was said, 'An eye for an eye and a tooth for a tooth,'" Jesus recalls. "But I say to you, do not [violently] resist one who does evil. If any one strikes you on the right cheek, turn to him the other as well. And if anyone orders you to go one mile, go two miles with him. Give to anyone who asks, and if anyone wants to borrow, do not turn away" [Mt 5:38-42]. Here, Jesus clearly advocates nonviolent resistance to evil, a new, third alternative to the methods of passive acceptance or active complicity in violence. Instead of passively accepting the oppressive and humiliating violence which lands on us like the back of a right hand slap across the face, we are to turn the cheek, look our oppressors in the eye, accept violence without retaliating. All the while we are to show our oppressors that we too are human, so that their hearts and eyes may be opened, the violence stopped and together we can become reconciled.[4]

If Jesus is clear about anything, it is his insistence that we are not to live in fear. The commandment, "Do not be afraid" appears exactly 365 times in the Bible, more than any other commandment of God. Likewise, the one message Jesus says to his terrified disciples over and over again, more than any other saying in all four Gospels, is "Do not be afraid." (See Matthew 10:31, 14:27, 28:10; Mark 5:36, 6:50; Luke 8:50, 12:7, 12:32; John 6:20.) Jesus knows how terrified we are, and he has compassion on us. That is why he touches us. He is gentle and kind. He gives us the best wisdom he has: "Rise, and do not be afraid."[5]

reflection questions

1. What fears have you faced and found to be unfounded?
2. How can you approach genuine threats to your security in life?
3. How much do you love God? Do you love God enough to abandon your fears and place your trust in God?
4. What changes can you make in your life to obey God's commandment to fear not?

scripture to ponder

Why are you so afraid, you of little faith? (Matthew 8:26, NIV)

[D]o not be afraid... (Matthew 10:31)

Do not fear, only believe. (Mark 5:36)

I can do all things through him [Christ] who strengthens me. (Philippians 4:13)

By the tender mercy of our God,
 the dawn from on high will break upon us,
to give light to those who sit in darkness and in the shadow of death,
 to guide our feet into the way of peace. (Luke 1:78-79)

Blessed are those who are persecuted for righteousness' sake, for theirs is the kingdom of heaven.

Blessed are you when people revile you and persecute you and utter all kinds of evil against you falsely on my account. Rejoice and be glad, for your reward is great in heaven, for in the same way they persecuted the prophets who were before you. (Matthew 5:10–12)

If any want to become my followers, let them deny themselves and take up their cross and follow me. For those who want to save their life will lose it, and those who lose their life for my sake will find it. For what will it profit them if they gain the whole world but forfeit their life? (Matthew 16:24–26)

57

concluding prayer

God, you see all that I am. You know my thoughts, my heart, what I say and what I do. I know you love me and I place my trust in you. Therefore, I do not fear any human being. I do not fear anything. I do not fear the power of death. Help me then to resist death and all the fears that bind human beings. Help me to break through human fear into true human relationships, into true solidarity with the poor and oppressed of the world, into voluntary poverty, into a deep, prayerful peace in my heart, into acts of nonviolence that can spark a transformation of the policies of death and oppression into food and housing for the poor. In the moment of confrontation, when I am publicly challenged, mocked or attacked, in those days ahead when I may be arrested and jailed for my nonviolent resistance, in those encounters when I embark on a new relationship with my oppressed sisters and brothers, in the hour of my death, let me pass from all fear to complete calm, peace, and trust rooted and grounded in you and your love. My daily prayer is: I shall fear no one. I shall place all my trust in You. I shall walk into the public world proclaiming my love for all people, especially the poor, resisting death and oppression and choosing life. I shall not be afraid. Jesus, I am coming. I will follow you. Receive me into your reign of love and peace.[6]

Notes

1 John Dear, *The Sound of Listening: A Retreat Journal from Thomas Merton's Hermitage* (New York: Continuum, 1999), p. 99.

2 John Dear, "Soldiers at My Front Door," wwwfatherjohndear.org; December 2003.

3 *Peace Behind Bars,* pp. 101–102.

4 John Dear, *The God of Peace: Toward a Theology of Nonviolence* (Eugene, Oreg.: Wipf and Stock, 1994), p. 23.

5 *Transfiguration,* p. 156

6 *Seeds of Nonviolence,* p. 147.

The Energy of Peace and Active Nonviolence

>...you will receive power when the Holy Spirit
>has come upon you; and you will be my
>witnesses...to the ends of the earth.
>
>—Acts 1:8

*T*o understand how to live
a life of active nonviolence, an understanding of the vocabulary of
peacemaking is necessary. A vital differentiation must be made
between pacifism (or active nonviolence) and passivity. At the root
of true pacifism is the desire to discover peaceful formulas for
addressing conflict at all levels. Yet pacifism in people's minds often
connotes passivity. Passivity, when related to peace seeking, indi-
cates lethargy, an inert state, a tendency to allow the world and its
tumultuous events to wash over one without consideration for what
might be done to make the world a more peaceful place. Passivity
leads to no positive resolution of the problems that abound in the
world. Because of the confusion associated with pacifism and passivity, John Dear and other notable peace seekers such as Mohandas
Gandhi and Martin Luther King, Jr., have preferred the term "active
nonviolence."

Active nonviolence is full of the energy of life and the creativity of humankind. It exudes a fervent desire for a better world. Active nonviolence searches, prays and works for alternatives to passivity or the destructive hatred that arises from injustice and violence.

How does one determine which course of life one is currently following or should follow? A passive view stems from believing that there is no hope. It is often paired with depression or despair. It drains energy and hobbles hope. Initially, when faced with a crisis, it is natural for a person to feel numb and unable to act. This is a normal first response but if that view persists, it's time to reassess. Active nonviolence, on the other hand, seeks ways to address the crisis situation through positive activity. Active nonviolence strives to defuse violence and certainly not to create additional hostile acts in response to a crisis. Retaliation cannot coexist with active nonviolence.

The grace of active nonviolence led parents of a murdered child to travel across the country to visit their child's murderer to offer forgiveness for an unthinkable crime. Following that incredible act of active nonretaliation, the couple offered their continuing friendship to the man in an attempt to bring life where death had reigned. Forgiveness frees. Certainly the couple will never be free of their great loss, but they are free of the devouring power of retaliation or passivity.

Forgiveness gives life. It restored a measure of life to the couple. It restored a bit of life to a man who would spend the remainder of his life in prison. Many would say he did not deserve to live, yet God calls the faithful to be life-giving not life-taking. The death penalty is life-taking. They represent acts of vengeance, which are beneath the call of the people of God. Certainly crimes must be addressed and the criminals brought to justice, but justice is not brought about through execution. Violence begets violence, and killing the guilty mocks true justice. When John asked Mother Teresa to contact a state governor to request clemency for a man on death row awaiting execution, Mother Teresa told the governor simply, "Do what Jesus would do." Her message is for our ears and our lives as well. *Do what Jesus would do.*

Personal defense experts remind us to breathe deeply if we are confronted by an attacker. Energy exists in that action, taking us to the source of our energy, the breath of life. We are energized with the power to think of peaceful ways to respond to a potentially violent act. Now may be the time for us to breathe deeply and confront any animosity we harbor against another group, person, nation or culture. That action is a means of regenerating our personal energy. Recognition of our need to forgive is the first step in forgiveness. As we realize our need to forgive, we choose to relinquish the hold that our unforgiveness has on us and the other person or group. Releasing the other frees us as it frees them. You might envision the energy required to cling to memories of past wrongs. Feel the stress and strain needed to hold on to animosity and hostility. It is the psychological and spiritual parallel to bearing a heavy burden for a lengthy distance over a difficult road. The longer the burden is borne, the wearier we become and the less energy we have for daily living.

thoughts from john

Peace begins within each of us. It is a process of repeatedly showing mercy to ourselves, forgiving ourselves, befriending ourselves, accepting ourselves, and loving ourselves. As we learn to appreciate ourselves and accept God's gift of peace, we begin to radiate peace and love to others.[1]

As the years go by, I find I need community more and more, including the experience of community among peace and justice groups across the country. In these grassroots communities, I find renewed energy and new friends who enrich my life.

If we want to live a life of peace, we need to risk new relationships. Widening the circle of communities that resist war and injustice, we expand the whole peace movement and together sound a stronger and clearer voice. Our lives bear more fruit than when we work alone.[2]

"We must develop and maintain the capacity to forgive," Martin Luther King, Jr., wrote. "The one who is devoid of the power to forgive is devoid of the power to love. Forgiveness is not an occasional act," King concluded. "It is a permanent attitude."[3]

The following was written during John's imprisonment for hammering on an F15E nuclear fighter bomber at Seymour Johnson Air Force Base, Goldsboro, N.C., December 7, 1993, in a symbolic act toward nuclear disarmament:

I read the Psalms tonight and dwell in God's presence. I pray for strength and grace. I ask for a deeper faith and a renewed hope that somehow my action, my imprisonment and my suffering will bear fruit for disarmament, justice and peace. May Jesus raise my spirit too.

As soon as I awake, a renewed strength comes over me. I do not know from where or how, but I am so grateful....My spirit has lifted. [4]

The following is a reflection on Matthew 14:22–33

Peacemaking is only possible for Christians if we keep our eyes focused on Jesus. As we remain centered in the peace of Christ, we can proceed with nonviolence, confronting militarism and oppression fearlessly. The moment we take our eyes off Jesus in our struggle for disarmament, justice and peace, the instant we start to let the winds of persecution and cultural criticism affect us, then our fears overtake us and we begin to sink. At that moment, we will not just be paralyzed with fear, we will be drowning in the turbulent sea.[5]

St. Ignatius Loyola, the founder of the Jesuits, urged his companions to take fifteen minutes at the end of every day for a prayerful review with God of that day, and in this way, ensure that one's heart is centered in God's peace as we fulfill our mission of doing justice. His *examen,* as he called it, can help us today as we seek to become a nonviolent people, centered in peace, responsible, committed to justice for the poor, willing to risk our very lives for our fellow human beings.

Begin by asking for light and understanding to see the day from God's perspective; then review the events of the day without judgment, and notice where I felt or saw the presence of God. Give thanks for those moments, and then reflect on those times when I failed to be at peace, when I was not nonviolent or loving, when I did things which I shouldn't have done and didn't do things which I should have done, for God's sake. Repent of those sins, ask for God's forgiveness, and pray for strength to be a better peacemaker for the next day. Ask God what God has to say to you about this day and that tomorrow. Conclude with a prayer of thanksgiving and resolve to be a better peacemaker the next day—more faithful, more nonviolent, more daring, more loving, more hopeful. This *examen,* Ignatius believed, with God's grace, would help us to become a people of peace.

Such is a spirituality for everyday peacemaking. Be rooted in a nonviolent love for all; be gentle with everyone, beginning with yourself; practice humility and kindness; accompany the poor and let go of possessions; join a community of peacemakers as they study the

Scriptures and seek the way of peace; speak the truth and act on it; say No to war and Yes to the Way of nonviolence, and accept the consequences—and most of all, be centered in God who calls us to be peacemakers, to be God's very sons and daughters. In this way, we will truly be blessed. Indeed, we will find ourselves dwelling in the house of God, the house of nonviolence.[6]

reflection questions

1. Do you frequently feel tired? Exhausted by news of conflict in the world? Tired by the challenging situations in your own life? How can you meet these challenges and walk with Jesus in the way of peace?

2. If you have ever held a grudge against another person, nation or culture, what effects did that ongoing unforgiveness create in you?

3. Consider a time when you forgave someone. Describe your feelings following your action. Did you feel energized? Free? Desiring to move forward with life?

4. Do you have the faith, courage and energy to get out of the boat of complacency and walk with Jesus on the waters of nonviolent action?

scripture to ponder

Peace I leave with you; my peace I give to you. I do not give to you as the world gives. Do not let your hearts be troubled, and do not let them be afraid. (John 14:27)

…the boat, battered by the waves, was far from the land, for the wind was against them. And early in the morning he [Jesus] came walking towards them on the lake. But when the disciples saw him walking on the lake, they were terrified, saying, "It is a ghost!" And they cried out in fear. But immediately Jesus spoke to them and said, "Take heart, it is I; do not be afraid."

Peter answered him, "Lord, if it is you, command me to come to you on the water." He said, "Come." So Peter got out of the boat, started walking on the water, and came towards Jesus. But when he noticed the strong wind, he became frightened, and beginning to sink, he cried out, "Lord, save me!" Jesus immediately reached out his hand and caught him, saying to him, "You of little faith, why did you doubt?" When they got into the boat, the wind ceased. And those in the boat worshiped him, saying, "Truly you are the Son of God." (Matthew 14:24–33)

May the God of hope fill you with all joy and peace in believing, so that you may abound in hope by the power of the Holy Spirit. (Romans 15:13)

Therefore, my beloved, just as you have always obeyed me, not only in my presence, but much more now in my absence, work out your own salvation with fear and trembling; for it is God who is at work in you, enabling you both to will and to work for his good pleasure. (Philippians 2:12–13).

May the God of peace himself sanctify you entirely, and may your spirit and soul and body be kept sound and blameless at the coming of our Lord Jesus Christ (1 Thessalonians 5:23)

concluding prayer

God, thank you for your great love and all that you give to me. Give me the grace and the courage to live a life of nonviolence so that I may be faithful to Jesus. Send me your Spirit that I may love everyone as my sister and brother and not fear anyone. Help me to be an instrument of your peace; to respond with love and not retaliate with violence; to accept suffering rather than inflict it; to live more simply; to resist death and to choose life for all your children. Guide me along

the way of nonviolence. Disarm my heart and I shall be your instrument to disarm other hearts. Lead me, God of nonviolence, into your
reign of love and peace, where there is no fear and no violence. In the
name of Jesus.[7] Amen.

Notes
1 *Living Peace,* p. 10.
2 *Living Peace,* p. 194.
3 *Living Peace,* p. 205, quoting Martin Luther King, Jr.
4 *Peace Behind Bars,* p. 79.
5 *Peace Behind Bars,* p. 97.
6 *Seeds of Nonviolence,* pp. 335–336.
7 *Just for Today,* Pax Christi brochure #534-047.

Retooling Our Hearts

> Love is patient; love is kind; love is not envious
> or boastful or arrogant or rude. It does not insist
> on its own way; it is not irritable or resentful;
> it does not rejoice in wrongdoing, but rejoices
> in the truth. It bears all things, believes all things,
> hopes all things, endures all things.
> Love never ends.
> —1 Corinthians 13:4–8

*J*esus came to proclaim a new way of living. One of the reasons Jesus' way has not worked is that it has never been truly applied to daily living by most of his followers for extended periods of history. Excuses abound for ignoring Jesus' way and following instead the way of contemporary culture. Practicality is a major obstacle to authentic Christian living. "You mean if a guy rams my car, I'm not supposed to get angry?" Of course, a crease in the fender or a shattered headlight will surely cause a moment of ire. What we do with our anger reveals whether our faith has seeped into our daily life. To threaten retaliation for an offense, large or small, is tantamount to throwing proverbial gasoline on the fire. We can come out swinging and raging, or we can come out thinking and praying about how best to handle the situation in a nonviolent manner. "Count to ten" is more than an old adage. It is a preliminary step to allowing our hearts to inform our brains which in turn informs our mouths, hands, our entire bodies about wise and appropriate ways to respond to a real, or sometimes an imagined, offense. The offending individual may seem like our enemy at the moment. That's when "Love your enemy" needs to be etched on our hearts for us to react in a Christian manner. "What would Jesus do?" we ask. Our message to ourselves if we are to be peacemakers must be, "I will do what Jesus would do."

An eye-for-an-eye mentality often supersedes loving one's enemies in today's world. It takes a quantum leap of faith truly to apply Jesus' way to our everyday way of life—without exception—so that all people do not end up "blind people." A fender dent may seem like a trite example of a need to retool our hearts, yet it is in the little things of life that the pattern of response is laid for the way in which larger events are resolved. If we succeed in retooling our own hearts to wise and calm responses to negative events, others around us will see and hopefully believe. As larger groups learn peacemaking skills, these people will become instruments of retooling hearts in their communities. The collective behavior of nations can be affected as the concentric circles of wisdom in facing adversity spread around the globe. It has been said that one person can make choices that affect the entire world. In fact, that is all that has ever brought about retooling of human hearts and actions. One person, one action, one retooling of our mind-set from anger or violence to nonviolent response initiates ongoing active nonviolence.

Prejudice may be built into our lives in subtle ways. Perhaps our immigrant family's past generations met many obstacles seeking job opportunities. Perhaps we often experience discrimination because of our sexual orientation, sex or race. Or perhaps we have to struggle to put food on the table and a roof over our heads, and we may be prejudiced against those with abundant financial resources. We cannot alter what we do not recognize and acknowledge. A rigorous heart search is required.

Retooling our hearts begins with a sincere desire to change our approach to adversity and to those who are different from us. "Lord, help me to become the person you have created me to be," might be our prayer for beginning the process. We can retool our hearts with prayer. Consider what the world would be like today, if, instead or retaliation, we all had prayed fervently without ceasing for a change of heart for Saddam Hussein or Osama bin Laden in the days preceding the wars in Iraq and Afghanistan?

thoughts from john

The gospel of Jesus calls us to love in a time of indifference, hope in a time of despair, nonviolence in a time of violence, justice in a time of injustice, and life in a time of death.[1]

"We have only just begun to practice the Gospel," Francis [of Assisi] told his followers as he died. Today we hear Francis tell us to embrace simplicity and poverty, serve those who are poor and needy, live in peace and nonviolence, love one another including our enemies, spend our days in contemplative prayer, and be devoted servants of Jesus and his Gospel. "While you are proclaiming peace with your lips," he wrote, "be careful to have it even more fully in your heart." He once explained, "If you own possessions, you need weapons to protect them and so we do not own anything and we are at peace with everyone." Francis' logic points the way toward personal, social, and global justice and peace. If each one of us practiced Gospel simplicity, voluntary poverty, and downward mobility, like Francis, we would share the world's resources with one another, have nothing to fear from others, and live in peace with everyone. If the whole world, especially the First World nations, practiced the Franciscan ethic of social justice and nonviolence, hunger and warfare would end. The U.S. comprises only 4% of the world's population, yet it controls over 60% of the world's natural resources. It maintains the world's largest arsenal of weapons, including 20,000 nuclear weapons, theoretically to prevent other nations from taking back the resources we have stolen from them. If we applied Francis' Gospel ethic toward ourselves, we would return the natural resources to the world's poor; relinquish the world's oil fields to their rightful owners, including Iraq; dismantle our nuclear weapons; and live in peace with everyone. In the process, we would learn, like Francis, to trust the God of peace.[2]

A spirituality for the life of peacemaking and doing justice entails a life of prayer and contemplation, a steady diet of reading the Scriptures, community worship and other prayer services, and also sitting quietly, in solitude, in God's peace. Peacemaking is a lifetime commitment. If I am going to be in it for the long haul—and the long haul keeps looking longer these days—I will need to drink daily from the well of prayer. This prayer helps me to focus on the truth of our peacemaking mission. Whether I am successful or not (and I cannot expect to improve on the crucified Jesus, a failure as far as the world is concerned), I can rest in peace knowing that our calling to be peacemakers is true, that God will use us to make peace.[3]

Those contemplative moments when we dwell in the peace that God offers us, can sustain us through the long days of peacemaking, and the long haul of living. In this light, we are able to see the world around us with new eyes, to look for God in all those we meet, and to see God in every human face. In this spirit, we can find God in the poor and in our enemies. We can encounter God in the nonviolent struggle for justice, in our daily life, in the world itself. In this spirit, we discover that God is alive, present, real, aware of us, loving us, calling us forever to dwell in peace and nonviolent love.

Spirituality develops as we let go of power and control, of the imperial ego that takes over our lives and prevents us from dwelling in God's peace. It emerges naturally as we take risks for peace—publicly, peacefully, lovingly—risks like opposing war, demanding housing for the poor, and speaking out against the death penalty. Be vulnerable before God and take the risk of peacemaking, the mystics tell us, and then God can use us as instruments of God's peace—in ways we never dreamed possible.... Not only can heartfelt prayer center us in God's peace, it will send forth a ripple of peace from us out into the world.[4]

How prayerful are we? How obedient to God? How awake? Do I pray that God's will be done, not mine, even if that means I must suffer?[5]

I recommend the following exercise as a way to develop contemplative nonviolence. Each morning, take thirty to sixty minutes sitting in silent meditation. Light a candle, read a scripture verse, and offer an opening prayer for God's blessing upon you and the world. Then, place yourself before Jesus or God as you imagine the gentle, loving God. Call to mind the person toward whom you hold a deep grudge, whoever stirs up feelings of anger, resentment, bitterness, or hatred. For some of us, there may be a long list of people who cause such feelings. We feel hurt by them, angry toward them, and bitter and resentful. Just pick one person. Tell Jesus about your anger, hatred, violence and resentment toward that person. Give those feelings to Jesus. Watch Jesus as he interacts with that person. Notice how he looks on that person with compassion, love, kindness, and truth. Why does Jesus show such deep compassion and kindness? Because that is the nature of God. Jesus is the love of God personified. He is the face of the God of nonviolence. He only knows compassion and nonviolent love. No matter how much violence, anger, resentment, or hatred we send his way, Jesus always responds with loving kindness, forgiveness, nonviolence, and compassion. In the process, he transforms us all. He saves us from our violence.[6]

We cannot idly pursue inner tranquillity while wars, bombings, executions, greed, and violence continue unchallenged. If we do not address the violence in the world, our inner peace is an empty illusion. Likewise, we cannot seek peace publicly and expect to help disarm the world while our hearts are filled with violence, judgment, and rage. Our work for peace cannot bear fruit if it is rooted in violence.[7]

reflection questions

1. How do you feel about the statistics that tell us that the U.S. comprises 4 percent of the world's population yet controls and uses over 60 percent of the planet's resources? How can this contribute to violence and suffering in the world?

2. Recall a time when you were able to love in a time of indifference, hope in a time of despair, act nonviolently and justly in a time of violence or injustice and discover life in a time of death. How did your reactions affect the situations in which you found yourself?

3. Think of a person who at the present seems to be an enemy rather than a friend. How does thinking of that individual make you feel? How can you alter your feelings?

scripture to ponder

[Jesus] said to them, 'Why are you afraid? Have you still no faith? (Mark 4:40)

[Love] does not insist on its own way; it is not irritable or resentful; it does not rejoice in wrongdoing, but rejoices in the truth. (1 Corinthians 13:5–6)

So if you have been raised with Christ, seek the things that are above, where Christ is, seated at the right hand of God. Set your minds on things that are above, not on things that are on earth, for you have died, and your life is hidden with Christ in God. When Christ who is your life is revealed, then you also will be revealed with him in glory. (Colossians 3:1–4)

You must understand this, that in the last days distressing times will come. For people will be lovers of themselves, lovers of money, boasters, arrogant, abusive, disobedient to their parents, ungrateful, unholy, inhuman, implacable, slanderers, profligates, brutes, haters of good, treacherous, reckless, swollen with conceit, lovers of pleasure rather than lovers of God, holding to the outward form of godliness but denying its power. Avoid them! (2 Timothy 3:1–5)

Show by your good life that your works are done with gentleness born of wisdom... the wisdom from above is first pure, then peaceable, gentle, willing to yield, full of mercy and good fruits, without a trace of partiality or hypocrisy. And a harvest of righteousness is sown in peace for those who make peace. (James 3:13, 17–18)

Finally, all of you, have unity of spirit, sympathy, love for one another, a tender heart, and a humble mind. Do not repay evil for evil or abuse for abuse; but, on the contrary, repay with a blessing. It is for this that you were called—that you might inherit a blessing.... Now who will harm you if you are eager to do what is good? But even if you do suffer for doing what is right, you are blessed. Do not fear what they fear, and do not be intimidated, but in your hearts sanctify Christ as Lord. Always be ready to make your defense to anyone who demands from you an account of the hope that is in you; yet do it with gentleness and reverence. (1 Peter 3:8–9, 13–16)

Therefore prepare your minds for action; discipline yourselves; set all your hope on the grace that Jesus Christ will bring you when he is revealed do not be conformed to the desires that you formerly had in ignorance. Instead, as he who called you is holy, be holy yourselves in all your conduct; for it is written, "You shall be holy, for I am holy." (1 Peter 1:13–16)

Rid yourselves, therefore, of all malice, and all guile, insincerity, envy, and all slander. (1 Peter 2:1)

Beloved, do not be surprised at the fiery ordeal that is taking place among you to test you, as though something strange were happening to you. But rejoice in so far as you are sharing Christ's sufferings, so that you may also be glad and shout for joy when his glory is revealed. (1 Peter 4:12–13)

…[w]henever you face trials of any kind, consider it nothing but joy, because you know that the testing of your faith produces endurance; and let endurance have its full effect, to that you may be mature and complete, lacking in nothing. (James 1:2–4)

c o n c l u d i n g   p r a y e r

Thank you, Lord Jesus, for bringing me here. Please come and stay intimately close to me. Shower me with your merciful love, your consoling presence, your abiding love, and, in doing so, transform me. If there may be some way, allow me to serve you and your people with loving-kindness and compassion, and to announce your reign of love by radiating it with my life. Use me in your peacemaking work to resist the principalities and powers of systemic violence; to proclaim the truth of nonviolence; to follow you along the way of the cross so that your redemptive work can continue through me, absorbing the world's hatred and violence and transforming it into mercy, reconciliation, and justice.

Lord, heal me, for I am broken and tired, restless and lost, bruised and hurt. I feel abandoned. I want to come home to you. Take me. Receive me. Grant me a new loving heart, a new inner peace, a life filled with joy, faith, hope, and love. Summon me to humble service and steadfast love toward others. May my life in you bear lasting fruit for humanity and all creation. Thank you for blessing me and the whole human family. I love you, O Christ.[8] Amen.

Notes

1 *Jesus the Rebel*, p. 193.
2 John Dear and William Hart McNichols, *You Will Be My Witnesses: Saints, Prophets and Martyrs* (Maryknoll, N.Y.: Orbis, 2006), pp. 45–46.
3 *Seeds of Nonviolence*, p. 331.
4 *Seeds of Nonviolence*, pp. 332–333.
5 *Peace Behind Bars*, p. 144.
6 *Mary of Nazareth*, p. 31.
7 *Living Peace*, pp. 14–15.
8 *The Sound of Listening*, p. 26.

reflection ten

Peace, the Only Option

> ...for God all things are possible.
> —Matthew 19:26

hen warring hordes scourged the steppes of Eurasia, attacking the civilizations of Eastern Europe in medieval times, the losses of humanity were great, the suffering severe. Yet the scorched lands healed, towns were rebuilt, new generations of babies born, civilization redeveloped. When settlers and native populations in North America clashed, European intruders destroyed the native peoples by conflict and disease. The lands of those native peoples who survived and whose progeny live today still have never been completely restored to them. However, many descendants of the colonists and the westward-moving pioneers acknowledge and confess the wrongs done to the original Americans and today respect the Native American heritage. World War I and World War II robbed the world of entire generations of its youth. Enemies in those conflicts subsequently became allies. The German city of Dresden, firebombed by the British in retaliation for attacks on Great Britain, rose from its ashes, though stark reminders of the horror remain emblazoned on the civilian population and on many of the city's structures.

With more than twenty thousand nuclear warheads stashed in the U.S. alone, the outcome of a full-scale nuclear war would hold little hope for healing, rebuilding or rebirth. Population centers would be vaporized with no regard for inhabitants. Retaliatory strikes would kill hundreds of thousands more. When no hostile authority remained to call for further attacks, the devouring of human, animal and all life would continue as clouds of radioactive material would swirl on the winds of the world deforming all life forms, mutating for all time the beautiful creation entrusted to humankind.

Impossible? No! John Dear writes,

"The Bomb makes every other issue redundant," Philip Berrigan told me when I interviewed him in 1992 for a peace journal. "The fact that we are complicit in the presence of the Bomb—because we help pay for it, we allow its deployment and possible use, and we have threatened to use it at least 25 times unilaterally during the last 47 years of the Cold War—destroys us spiritually, morally, psychologically, emotionally and humanly. Our complicity in the Bomb makes us incapable of dealing with lesser social and political problems that are in reality spin-offs of our dedication to the bomb."[1]

History has revealed what violence can accomplish. The cities of Hiroshima and Nagasaki remain scarred with the effects of the atomic bomb. More tragically, the surviving *hibakusha* (those affected by the explosions), who live with the scars both physically, emotionally and spiritually each day of their lives, are reminders of a violent response to a violent action. Some historians state that bombing these Japanese cities and incinerating their people was unnecessary, arguing that the war against Japan had basically already been won. The decision to annihilate a people was made in order to make a statement that the U.S. was the dominant power on earth.[2]

More recently retaliatory aggression to avenge the tragic deaths of three thousand-plus Americans in the 9/11 attacks on the World Trade Center and the Pentagon and the hijacking of Flight 93 have led to the additional deaths of more than four thousand Americans and those of other participating nations [as of this writing] in a war against not those who perpetrated the 9/11 attacks, but against innocent children, women and men in Iraq and Afghanistan. War does not pave the path to peace.

Complicated rivalries bloody many continents. In Africa the tragedy of conflict in Darfur has claimed over four hundred thousand lives [as of this writing]. Hutus in Rwanda were hacked and maimed by their Tutsi neighbors before the massacres ceased. I witnessed a Catholic Relief Services worker's grief describing her harrowing experiences in Sierra Leone as she watched workers shoveling the severed arms and legs of victims of civil war into truckbeds. This woman would go on with her mission to assist other people of impoverished countries. A young Rwandan priest told how he had lost every member of his family in the slaughter in his country. He had been spared because he was studying in Rome. When I asked what he would do when his studies were complete, he responded calmly, "I'll go home to Rwanda. They are my people." Asia has suffered under the Korean War, the horrors of Vietnam, the killing fields of Cambodia, and have witnessed many horrors such as the beatings of gentle Buddhist monks attempting to stand against the violence against their land and their people.

No one ever truly wins such conflicts. The price paid by those who lose the war is obvious...death, mutilation, poverty, powerlessness, anguish. Perhaps an even greater price is paid by those who appear to win. They are faced with pride, arrogance, ill-founded faith in violence, loss of compassion, guilt, a need to defend what was taken by force, the loss of true faith. The self-inflicted injuries, number of suicides, and attempted suicides plus incredibly high numbers of returning military persons affected by Post-Traumatic Stress Disorder (PTSD) from our current and past wars bears witness to the price paid by those in combat zones.

It seems incomprehensible that the nation that dropped the bomb, not once but twice, labels other countries that attempt to develop nuclear weapons as "evil empires." It is mind-boggling to consider that the nation that attacked Iraq searching for weapons of mass destruction (which did not exist) is the nation that harbors more than twenty thousand weapons of mass nuclear destruction in its own arsenal. The U.S. continues to develop and stockpile thousands of nuclear weapons, a few of which could annihilate the world as we know it. Even if the armaments are never deployed, the devastation they wreak upon the land and the health of the people who live around the production sites at Los Alamos is tragic. Peace should be our "war" cry. Peace is the only option in a world bristling with nuclear potential for the incineration of all of civilization.

From time to time in the writing of this book the thought would trouble me, "Is peace actually possible?" Always the response that came from deep within my being was, "With God all things are possible." Ultimately, only the peace of God can save our civilization. Only God can lead us to peace. We must trust in the Prince of Peace, in the God of peace and act in accord with that trust.

thoughts from john

As we have seen from the abolitionist, suffragist, civil rights, antiwar, human rights, and environmental movements, patient grassroots organizing and reconciliation over time has the power to transform nations and the world.

I believe that if we want to explore the horizons of peace, we need to join with organizations and nonviolent movements striving to transform the world. As we add our voices to these programs and sow the seeds of peace and reconciliation, we become part of a movement larger than ourselves, and thus take our part in history's journey to peace.[3]

Gaudium et Spes ("The Pastoral Constitution on the Church in the Modern World"), ratified on December 7, 1965, issued a breathtaking new vision for the church. It threw wide the doors of the church, looked out on the world, affirmed humanity in its "joys and hopes, its griefs and anguishes," and called forth a new vision of love, human community and justice. It dealt with a plethora of topics: truth, conscience, freedom, death, atheism, the common good, the human person, social justice, solidarity, marriage, culture, economics, work and property. In particular, however, it issued the only condemnation of the Second Vatican Council, a condemnation of nuclear war....

Jesus' command to love enemies is restated as a foundational mandate....the document "outlined the true and noble nature of peace, condemned the savagery of war, and earnestly exhorted Christians to cooperate with all in securing a peace based on justice and charity."[4]

Every moment offers us God's invitation to live in God's own peace. Wherever we are, we can reject violence and war, and take up the exciting journey by proclaiming God's reign of peace here on earth.

The challenge is to start the journey, to stay faithful, and to delve into a life of peace. Though there will be many days when the journey will seem futile, daunting, even hopeless, over time we come to realize that the journey itself is the life of peace! All we have to do is choose to take up that journey and stay faithful.[5]

Last week, I drove up the mountain to the town of Los Alamos, birthplace of the bomb, along Trinity Drive past Oppenheimer Road near the National Nuclear Weapons Labs. I was there for a very unusual speaking invitation— to talk about peace and disarmament to a group of students at Los Alamos High School. I approached the doors with a vague sense of dread, but left exhilarated. These bright young students gave me hope.

Los Alamos is one eerie place. Situated atop gorgeous red and orange mesas, it's by all appearance a basic American town. It has all the usual amenities—a bank, a library, a grocery store, a Starbucks, a large Endoscopy center. And then again a few things most towns lack—tons of radioactive waste and laboratories from which spring the latest nuclear weapons capable of vaporizing millions.

And another deep contradiction. At the Immaculate Heart of Mary Church—a beautiful pond out front, a statue of St. Francis and a stone bench dedicated to Mother Teresa—the priest blesses the Bomb and tells lab employees they are doing God's will.

Los Alamos has the feel of the 1950s film, "The Invasion of the Body Snatchers," where the people have vanished and in their place are their exact replicas, but without soul or spirit. Los Alamos is like that. Most people shuffle through town like zombies, going mindlessly to work, heartlessly doing their jobs, preparing for the destruction of the planet. Los Alamos is a soulless place.

Massive denial prevails. Most will not acknowledge that their work portends the end of the world. And thus they confirm Gandhi's wisdom. He said the Bomb destroyed Japanese bodies; it will come to destroy American souls.

Down the street from the labs stands Los Alamos High School. Located in one of the poorest states in the nation, yet centered in the nation's wealthiest counties—this according to the *Santa Fe New Mexican*. Most students' parents work at the Labs, and they make a fortune.

And thus my trepidation. What reception was I to expect? But my worries were put at rest. Megan, a bright young senior, greeted me warmly and said she was happy to be my host. She walked me through the school and explained that she could not tell the faculty or the principal that I was coming because my talk would have been banned. I understood and nodded. The people of Los Alamos haven't taken kindly to me, particularly the Catholics there.

Megan and her friends recently formed the Peace and Global Concerns Club. Last month, to mark the fifth anniversary of the U.S. war on Iraq, 20 of them announced they would stage a walkout. The principal threatened to suspend them all, but the students went ahead with their plan. When the moment arrived, 150 students walked out of classes and sat for two hours on the lawn in front of the school holding anti war signs.

Their action made the front page of the *Los Alamos Monitor*, and caused a debate throughout the community. The principal backed down; no one was suspended.

Megan escorted me to the room and there I found 25 eager students ready to engage me in a discussion of peace, disarmament, nonviolence and justice. I shared my stories, explained the urgent need to dismantle our nuclear arsenal and practice nonviolent conflict resolution, and I pointed to the spiritual roots of peacemaking and the invitation of the God of peace.

And how impressed I was with these students. Their attention was earnest and serious. These are kids growing up in the shadow of the Bomb, whose parents earn their living preparing the destruction of the planet, in a town where the churches bless nuclear weapons and cancer has become the norm. Yet in all this they formed a conscience and then a peace group. No small accomplishment.

They listened attentively then asked questions: What should we do? How do you begin to work for peace? What would real security look like anyway? How do we reach that tipping point? And then their spectacular insights: You're talking about a world of nonviolence, but aren't you really pointing us to a world without fear? Is the quest for peace impossible without an inner search for God?

They astonished me. Their faces were so searching, their questions deep and serious. One of them told me, she grew up hearing that the lab employees were the greatest peacemakers in the nation. Case closed. Still, she asked the hard questions; she pondered the critical link. Obscene armaments steal food from the tables of the poor. These students understood more than most the realities of nuclear weapons.[6]

The world spends nearly a trillion dollars each year on weapons of death. Though we produce enough food to feed adequately more than the current global population, 950,000,000 people are chronically malnourished. Six thousand people, primarily children, die each day from starvation, while the best and brightest minds of the world's governments spend their energies and the world's resources on the business of war. Forty million people worldwide die each year from starvation and preventable diseases. A child dies of hunger and hunger-related causes approximately every two seconds. Some fourteen million children die yearly of preventable disease. An additional 1.5 million children were killed in wars worldwide in the 1980s.

Despite this forced, institutionalized suffering that affects so many human beings, global expenditures on arms and armies approach one trillion dollars a year—about two million dollars a minute—an amount that easily could reduce worldwide starvation, disease and poverty if it were spent on services for the world's poor. World military expenditures from 1960 to 1990 add up to twenty-one trillion dollars ($21,000,000,000,000) in 1987 US dollars, equivalent in size to the value of all goods and services produced by and for the 5.3 billion people on the earth in the year 1990.

Since 1500, when the history of war began to be recorded, there have been 589 "official" wars, and 141,901,000 people have been killed in these wars. In the twentieth century, there have been over four times as many war deaths as in the four hundred years preceding. During the 1980s the number of wars reached an all-time peak and three-fourths of the people killed in them were civilians. The world now has twenty-six million people in the regular armed forces, another forty million in military reserves, and sixty-four national governments under some form of explicit military control. In the early 1990s over forty wars were being fought simultaneously around the world.

With the atomic bombings of Hiroshima on August 6, 1945, and Nagasaki on August 9, 1945, the destruction of the entire human race and the planet itself has become possible.[7]

reflection questions

1. Consider alternatives to peace that exist in your personal life and in the world. What are their implications if followed for years to come?

2. If you find it difficult to accept the concept of peace as the only option for the future of the world, visualize the world that would result if violence continues and escalates. How would you respond to such a world?

3. The Peace Prayer attributed to Saint Francis of Assisi asks, "Lord, make me an instrument of your peace." What is one thing you can do on a daily basis to allow God to make you an instrument of peace in your corner of the world?

scripture to ponder

O LORD, you will ordain peace for us,
for indeed, all that we have done, you have done for us. (Isaiah 26:12)

Put things in order... live in peace; and the God of love and peace will be with you. (2 Corinthians 13:11)

Cast all your anxiety on him, because he cares for you. (1 Peter 5:7)

Do not let your hearts be troubled. (John 14:1)

If you love me, you will keep my commandments. And I will ask the Father, and he will give you another Advocate, to be with you for ever. This is the Spirit of truth, whom the world cannot receive, because it neither sees him nor knows him. You know him, because he abides with you, and he will be in you. (John 14:15–17).

Be still, and know that I am God! (Psalm 46:10)

concluding prayer

Dear Jesus,

Help me to go down the mountain [of Transfiguration] with you and accompany you on the way of the cross, that I too might confront and resist systemic injustice with your loving nonviolence, that I too might accept suffering with love and forgiveness and not a trace of revenge or retaliation in the struggle for justice, that I too might enter the new life of resurrection.

Help me to pray and fast, that I might expel the demons of war and death from others and heal others to live in the Holy Spirit of love and life.

Heal me that I might always walk beside you on the path of love, nonviolence, and peace.

Make me your faithful disciple and friend to transform our anti-transfiguration world of war, violence, and nuclear weapons, that we might all welcome your reign of peace and love.[8] Amen.

Notes

1 John Dear, "Prophets of Peace and Justice: Moral Leadership in a Culture of War" in *Faith Seeking Understanding: Moral Leadership*, vol. 3, Fall, pp. 23–24.

2 In an address to Greenpeace during the commemoration of the sixtieth anniversary of the US bombings of Japan, Mark Seldon, a historian from Cornell University of Ithaca, New York and Peter Kuznick, director of the Nuclear Studies Institute at American University in Washington, D.C., argued that the U.S. decision to drop atomic bombs on Hiroshima and Nagasaki in 1945 was meant to kick-start the Cold War rather than end the Second World War, and was done more to impress the Soviet Union than to defeat Japan. They also argued that President Harry Truman was culpable for the large human death toll. For more information see "Hiroshima Bomb May Have Carried Hidden Agenda," www.NewScientist.com. Additionally, John Dear recommends reading historians Gar Alperovitz and Kai Bird, and William D. Leahy's *I Was There: The Personal Story of the Chief of Staff to President Roosevelt and Truman.*

3 *Living Peace*, p. 213.

4 *The God of Peace*, p. 116.

5 *Living Peace*, p. 79.

6 John Dear, "On the Road to Peace," "A Visit to Los Alamos High School" May 8, 2008. www.johndear.org.

7 *The God of Peace*, p. 7.

8 *Transfiguration*, pp. 206–207.

reflection eleven

The Future of Peace

> Be careful then how you live, not as unwise
> people but as wise, making the most of
> the time, because the days are evil. So do
> not be foolish, but understand what
> the will of the Lord is.
> —Ephesians 5:15–17

When one views the future of peace through the media of newspapers and television, the outlook seems grim. Even a historical view can paint an ominous picture unless one looks deeply into the transforming periods of history. The future of peace is intrinsically linked to our own personal futures.

Following World War II the Iron Curtain of Soviet influence shadowed the world with fear and shrouded the people who lived behind it in isolation and oppression. The Berlin Wall separated neighbors and families. During the 1950s, communities and families in the U.S. constructed bomb shelters. Schools conducted emergency drills and procedures for bomb attacks, fearing that nuclear attack from the Soviet Union was imminent. Many citizens of the U.S. then and now failed to recognize that fear had been created when the U.S. exploded the bombs in Japan at the conclusion of World War II. A dangerous model had been set into motion. The potential for nuclear annihilation had entered history.

Yet history did not bear out these particular fears at that time. Eventually, the Iron Curtain lifted; the Berlin Wall came down in rubble. All this occurred without overt warfare. Perhaps the erosion of the Iron Curtain was the result of a different kind of warfare, prayer warfare, as prayers for the salvation of Russia were raised to God for decades.

After the collapse of the Soviet Union amazing stories emerged of the survival of faith in a godless society. Older people and religious groups had not surrendered their faith but had nurtured it amid the most adverse conditions. As religious practices were forced underground, many responded with deepened faith. Jesus has promised, "I will be with you always." The endurance of those whose faith had been suppressed bears witness to the truth of Jesus' promise. The future of peace today is sustained by that same promise. If we choose to follow the path of peace, Jesus will accompany us all the way.

A Native American was attempting to explain to his grandchildren what it was like to be an elder among their people. "It takes strength," he said. "I feel like I have two wolves fighting in my heart. One is mean, angry, violent, wanting revenge. The other wolf is kind and loving and full of compassion."

"Which wolf will win this fight?" asked one of the children.

"The one I feed," the man replied.

Perhaps the future of peace will be determined by which "wolf" we feed through our daily activities. We have a choice: to feed the fear, anger and vengeance that rises when events in the world seem to be out of control or to feed the sense of hope and compassion with a spirit of true justice and active nonviolence when faced with difficult circumstances. Which will we choose?

thoughts from john

The gospel of Jesus calls us to love in a time of indifference, hope in a time of despair, nonviolence in a time of violence, justice in a time of injustice, and life in a time of death. Jesus teaches us not only how to live but how to die; how to transform not only the world but our own broken hearts as well; not only how to believe but in whom to believe.

In the end, Jesus the rebel shows us the face of God. His revolution transcends all our hopes for a better world for, in Jesus, the reign of God is at hand, here and now, at this very moment in human history. All people are created and destined for that reign of love and mercy, where our beloved God dwells.

In Jesus, we meet our beloved God. From now on we know that our God is not a god of despair but the God of hope; not a god of wrath but the God of mercy; not a god of condemnation but the God of compassion; not a god of imperial power but the God of the cross; not a god of domination but the God of loving service; not a god of oppression but the God of liberation; not a god who blesses injustice but the God of justice; not a god of war but the God of peace; not a god of violence but the God of nonviolence; not a god of death but the God of Life. From now on we know that we have been created to share in the fullness of life, in God's own life of love and unending mercy. [1]

We have been changed forever, God has begun the revolution within us. We are sent out into the world as ambassadors of that revolutionary, nonviolent God. God sends us to prepare a new world for God right here on earth. Alive in faith, we take up the journey to nonviolent love. Our prayer is constant: "Come, Lord Jesus."[2]

"The Christian ideal has not been tried and found wanting," Chesterton wrote long ago. "It has been found difficult and left untried." Our Gospel heralds a hard but beautiful message. It demands dedication to the poor and a committed struggle for justice. Luke suggests that if we heed the message of Moses and the prophets—indeed, if we accept the resurrection of Christ—then we will live serving others as the Good Samaritan did, as Jesus did. Not only will we relieve the suffering of the poor and comfort the afflicted, we will give our lives for the struggle for justice and peace.[3]

Each one of us is summoned to fulfill this great mission. God is leading us on our journey through life to accomplish God's work of compassionate love and disarming peace. When we finally meet God face-to-face, we will understand the mission that had been given to us, and realize that we were never alone, that we had nothing to fear, and that all we had to do was be faithful to the discipleship journey and the work of transfiguration nonviolence.[4]

"Behold, I am the servant of God," Mary tells the angel [at the Annunciation]. "Let it be with me according to your word."

With that yes, the story of Jesus begins. God becomes human. We humans learn first hand about God. Everything can change for the better, if we only heed the invitation.

But Mary's yes could not have been easy. Even though she is a young, frightened girl, there must have been a hard-fought inner life of prayer and peacemaking for her to move from fear and confusion to humble acceptance of God's will. According to various scripture scholars, including a leading feminist theologian, a better translation of Mary's answer would be, "Behold, I am the slave of God." The Greek word implies that Mary sees herself not just as a servant, but as God's slave. In this politically incorrect description, Mary obeys the orders of her master. As a slave, she has no real personal life; she suffers by doing whatever the master requires of her. Her obedience is complete. There is no other alternative.

The saints of history, from Paul of Tarsus to Dorothy Day, testify that real obedience to God leads to redemptive suffering and love, and from there, to the mystical experience of freedom. The "slave's obedience" to God somehow is not violent, but in the end, life-giving, liberating, transforming, leading to the depths of love and peace. Obedience to God leads ultimately to joy because it leads to God.[5]

reflection questions

1. How does the future of peace appear differently to you after considering these reflections?

2. How can you help prepare your little corner of the world for the journey to nonviolent love?

3. What participation in active nonviolence might you join to brighten the future of peace in our world?

4. How might you respond to those who claim that violence is necessary to protect ourselves?

5. If the future of peace still seems bleak to you, what steps can you take to trust God's care for our world?

6. In 1998, Nobel peace laureates were invited by the United Nations to commit to educating the world's children in the ways of peace. The General Assembly declared 2001–2010 to be a "Decade for a Culture of Peace and Nonviolence for the Children of the World." Has that been achieved? If not, how can you help educate children in the ways of peace for future decades?

scripture to ponder

Now faith is the assurance of things hoped for, the conviction of things not seen. (Hebrews 11:1)

[I]f my people who are called by my name humble themselves, pray, seek my face, and turn from their wicked ways, then I will hear from heaven, and will forgive their sin and heal their land. (2 Chronicles 7:14)

concluding prayer

Dear Jesus,

Please help me to fulfill my mission on earth, that I might join you in your mission of transfiguration nonviolence, that I might accompany you in your work to disarm, transform, heal, and redeem humanity.

Make me an instrument of your love and peace.

Disarm my heart and send me forth into the world of war and violence that I might disarm othersand welcome your reign of peace and nonviolence.

Help me to live each moment in peace.

Help me never to hurt another person again.

Give me the grace to resist and transform the structures of violence, to help build a global grassroots movement of transfiguration nonviolence, so that one day we might abolish war, injustice, poverty, and nuclear weapons, and everyone might live in the light of your transfiguration peace.[6] Amen.

Notes

1 *Jesus the Rebel,* p. 193.
2 *Jesus the Rebel,* p. 194.
3 *Jesus the Rebel,* p. 102.
4 *Transfiguration,* p. 230.
5 *Mary of Nazareth,* pp. 43–44.
6 *Transfiguration,* pp. 232–233.

Jesus, the Prince of Peace

> For a child has been born for us,
> a son given to us;
> authority rests upon his shoulders;
> and he is named
> Wonderful Counselor, Mighty God,
> Everlasting Father, Prince of Peace.
> His authority shall grow continually,
> and there shall be endless peace
> for the throne of David and his kingdom.
> He will establish and uphold it
> with justice and with righteousness
> from this time onward and for evermore.
> The zeal of the LORD of hosts will do this.
> —Isaiah 9:6–7

*P*eace is impossible...if we attempt to find it, create it or secure it on our own. The good news is that we are not expected to venture into peace negotiations with the world, or even ourselves or our families, alone. Each hope, each thought, each move, each action we make toward seeking genuine peace finds us walking with the Prince of Peace, Jesus.

When we walk into difficult or threatening circumstances, when we confront the grave injustices of our time, we can visualize Jesus, the Prince of Peace, walking beside us or, we hope, leading our way. That act may produce an image of the physical presence of Jesus at our side, but more importantly, it expresses the spiritual truth that Jesus is always with us. Visualization only makes that presence more viable to our physical being and our intellectual understanding. That presence will lead us to work toward establishing justice so that peace can grow from those roots. John reminds us:

> Today there are so many areas of injustice it's hard to know where to begin. Racism, sexism, poverty, and oppression flourish around the world. We cannot personally solve every injustice, but we can't just sit back and allow injustice to continue. Whether we struggle for an end to racism or sexism, for the rights of the people of Sudan or the homeless, for an end to torture or for a living wage, we can make a positive contribution that will move us all toward social, racial, political, and economic justice.[1]

To that list of injustices in need of challenge and change we might add the rights of the unborn and the inclusion of all people regardless of sexual orientation or religious persuasion. Jesus came for everyone. People will not be drawn to his way of life by being reviled and brutalized for who they are. Conversion comes through the overwhelming knowledge that God loves us—all of us—and that God sent Jesus as our Savior, to bring us back from the brink of doom brought about by sin. In reality, there is only one sin: turning away from God. And there is simply one conversion: returning to God's love as shown through Jesus the Christ, Jesus the Prince of Peace.

Isaiah's prophecy reminds us that the road to peace winds through a multitude of pathways: establishing and upholding justice, righteousness from now into times called "evermore." The trip began for zeal of the Lord. That zeal for the Lord's way is within us. Our call is to set the way free in the world.

The inner life of peace means acting from a deep conviction about who we are, that each one of us is a beloved child of God, a human being called to love and serve other human beings. Living from this conviction does not mean we ignore our emotions—quite the contrary. In fact, as we go forward into the world, to places like death row, soup kitchens, or war zones, we touch the pain of the world and feel the full range of human emotions, with sorrow and anger, as we experience the pain of human tragedy and injustice. In 1985, while living in a refugee camp in El Salvador's war zone, I felt terrible sorrow, grief, and outrage as I witnessed the death and destruction around me, but I also felt a great inner peace because I clung to my faith in the God of peace, who seemed palpably present in the suffering people around me. Deep down, I rested in God's peace and even felt joy while I endured and resisted the horror of war with the refugees around me.[2]

Peace can be found in the most astonishing places and times; John describes his experience in the aftermath of the September 11 attacks:

I remember one Catholic mother who came to Ground Zero to find closure over the loss of her son, hoping the trip would bear her along. She gazed over the towering wreckage and wept awhile. Then, back on the boat, she looked me in the eye and whispered, "I have no room for anger."

I was astonished at her strength. The ground rules had been set by our president, and the media had made things clear: This woman's role was to call for blood. She was supposed to be angry and vengeful. But no, this mother kept her heart to herself and let it lead the way, a path forged by grief, conscience, and love. "I feel only compassion for the families of the hijackers," she said. "Imagine what suffering they must have known to produce such violence. What must their families be going through?" With that, she rejected out of hand any sort of retaliation. "Bombing Afghanistan will never bring my son back," she concluded, stating what no one else dared to state. "It will only add to my grief." Hers was a greatness I rarely encountered in anyone during those days.[3]

Companionship with Jesus is the essence of the matter. There's no denying the truth of John's Gospel: "Just as a branch cannot bear fruit on its own...neither can you unless you remain in me.... It was not you who chose me, but I who chose you" (John 15:4, 5, 16). I take this to heart and try to keep it close. I do it through time-honored ways: daily meditation, Bible study, life in community, service, sacraments, and solidarity with the poor. My disciplines still teach me about Jesus and fortify my discipleship to him.[4]

Most of us admire Jesus, but none of us want to undergo what he suffered, to make that journey to Jerusalem and that last, uphill climb to Calvary. In this age of pop stars and movie celebrities, we are, at best, fans of Jesus, not followers. But discipleship means walking in his footsteps from Galilee to Tabor then to Jerusalem, where Jesus turns over the tables of imperial injustice and faces arrest and execution. We may go to church, we may read the Gospels, we may respect his teachings, but to follow Jesus faithfully means to turn toward our own modern-day Jerusalems, resisting systemic injustice, putting down our swords, forgiving those who hurt us, and taking up the cross of nonviolent, suffering love in the struggle for justice and peace.

Since Jesus defended the poor, confronted injustice, challenged the ruling authorities, and broke every unjust law, his journey could only lead to a showdown with the imperial powers. Because we are his followers, our Gospel journey to peace and justice will also get us in trouble. Our discipleship to Jesus will lead us to love our neighbors, love our enemies, defend the poor, denounce injustice, break unjust laws, oppose war, and confront institutionalized violence with active non-violence. Discipleship will disrupt our lives and take us down a path not of comfort and consolation but of pain and sacrifice. At some point, we too will want to climb a mountain in search of prayerful solitude with our beloved God.

Dietrich Bonhoeffer wrote long ago that the problem with Christians today is that we do not want to pay the price for following Jesus. We want "cheap grace," not the costly grace of the Gospel. Because we want cheap grace, we end up with all the trappings of church, power, ritual, and religious legalism, everything but Jesus and a living discipleship to him here and now in our own lives.[5]

reflection questions

1. How can you do what John suggests in order to do what Jesus would do?

Heal those around you. Pray and fast for those in need. Touch the marginalized and oppressed with your compassionate love. Expel the demons of violence and death, and help others live in the Holy Spirit of love and peace.[6]

Allow Christ to disarm your heart; commit yourself to Gospel non-violence; and live today in the light of his peace, love, and compassion.[7]

How can you connect your life more and more to the mission of Jesus, so that you too live a life of unconditional love, boundless compassion, creative nonviolence, steadfast resistance to evil, and perfect peace toward everyone?[8]

How can you help humanity "beat swords into plowshares" and "study war no more"? What blocks you from being more loving and compassionate, from working for peace and justice?[9]

2. How can you make your life story fit the life story of Jesus?

scripture to ponder

Suddenly, one of those with Jesus put his hand on his sword, drew it, and struck the slave of the high priest, cutting off his ear. Then Jesus said to him, "Put your sword back into its place; for all who take the sword will perish by the sword." (Matthew 26:51–52)

Then Jesus said, "Father, forgive them; for they do not know what they are doing." (Luke 23:34)

While they were talking about this, Jesus himself stood among them and said to them, "Peace be with you." They were startled and terrified, and thought that they were seeing a ghost. He said to them, "Why are you frightened, and why do doubts arise in your hearts?" (Luke 24:36–38)

Jesus came and stood among them and said, "Peace be with you." After he said this, he showed them his hands and his side. Then the disciples rejoiced when they saw the Lord. Jesus said to them again, "Peace be with you. As the Father has sent me, so I send you." When he had said this, he breathed on them and said to them, "Receive the Holy Spirit." (John 20:19–22)

concluding prayer

In the name of the God of peace... the nonviolent Jesus, and the Holy Spirit of Love.[10] Amen.

Notes
1 *Living Peace,* p. 165.
2 *Living Peace,* p. 14.
3 *A Persistent Peace,* p. 351.
4 *A Persistent Peace,* p. 80.
5 *Transfiguration,* pp. 62–63.
6 *Transfiguration,* p. 162.
7 *Transfiguration,* p. 161.
8 *Transfiguration,* pp. 231–232.
9 *Transfiguration,* p. 67.
10 *A Persistent Peace,* p. 234.

The Chapter You Write With Your Life

Not everyone who says to me, "Lord, Lord,"
will enter the kingdom of heaven, but only one
who does the will of my Father in heaven....
—Matthew 7:21

*B*y word and example Father John Dear has provided many thoughts for living a gospel life of active nonviolence. Now is the time to reflect on how your life can be shaped in the way of nonviolence, the Way of Jesus, who is the Prince of Peace. You have reached a change-point time of decision. To believe or not believe the call to active nonviolence as the call to follow Jesus is at hand. Following Jesus is not easy—it never has been—though we have camouflaged the reality of the difficulty of the journey with a spirituality of sweet baby Jesus at Christmas and a focus on the Resurrection without fully absorbing the pain and sacrifice of the Crucifixion at Easter. Each step of Jesus' journey on earth leaves footprints for us to follow...or to not follow. The choice is ours. It is perfectly OK to begin with baby steps, perhaps in the way that one tests the water of the ocean or a pool before plunging in. Just dip in a bit to see how it feels to enter the world of active nonviolence. You will find companions and support. You may be surprised by whom and how many. Sometimes the voices of the doves of peace are drowned out by the hawks of war simply because the doves may be soft-spoken, gentle people. But gentle does not mean weak. Gentleness bears great strength.

Prayer is without doubt the only way to wend one's way along the road of peace. Read and reread the Scriptures cited in the previous reflections. Pray the Scriptures. Imagine yourself within the happenings and admonitions of those words. Discover which passages speak to you most clearly. They may be the ones that you find yourself resisting the most. That's OK. Listen to them! Move in the direction they lead you.

Now John offers a prayer for you as you ponder your future in the realm of active nonviolence.

Thank you, Lord Jesus, for bringing me here. Please come and stay intimately close to me. Shower me with your merciful love, your consoling presence, your abiding love, and, in doing so, transform me. If there may be some way, allow me to serve you and your people with loving-kindness and compassion, and to announce your reign of love by radiating it with my life. Use me in your peacemaking work to resist the principalities and powers of systemic violence; to proclaim the truth of nonviolence; to follow you along the way of the cross so that your redemptive work can continue through me, absorbing the world's hatred violence and transforming it into mercy, reconciliation, and justice.

Lord, heal me, for I am broken and tired, restless and lost, bruised and hurt. I feel abandoned. I want to come home to you. Take me. Receive me. Grant me a new loving heart, a new inner peace, a life filled with joy, faith, hope, and love. Summon me to humble service and steadfast love toward others. May my life in you bear lasting fruit for humanity and all creation. Thank you for blessing me and the whole human family. I love you, O Christ.[1] Amen.

reflection questions

1. How do you identify yourself? What gives you your identity? What would it mean for you to see yourself first and foremost in relationship with Jesus, as a disciple and companion of Jesus?[2]
2. What is your prayer for yourself?
3. What is your prayer for the world?

scripture to ponder further

_____

_____

_____

_____

_____

_____

concluding prayer

Come, Holy Spirit, send your driving wind upon us and blow away the cobwebs in our hearts and minds and give us the fresh air of the breath of Jesus.

Come, Holy Spirit, send your blazing fire upon us so that we may burn with love and compassion for each other and love every human being everywhere.

Come, Holy Spirit, give us new tongues to speak the good news of peace, justice and nonviolence to a world of war, injustice and violence.

Come, Holy Spirit, send us into the streets, into the world, to share the love of God with one another, to talk about the nonviolent Jesus, to denounce the evil spirits of violence, greed, war, injustice, greed, empire and death. And then to proclaim Jesus' reign of love, mercy, disarmament, justice, nonviolence and reconciliation.

Come, Holy Spirit, fill us with the joy of Christ, so that no matter what we're going through, no matter our problems, we may always live in you.

Come, Holy Spirit, make us instruments of your peace. Help us to carry on the Acts of the Apostles. Make us heralds of a new world without war, poverty, nuclear weapons or global warming, a new world of love, nonviolence, justice and peace.[3] Amen.

Notes
1 *Transfiguration*, p. 26.
2 *Transfiguration*, p. 67.
3 "The Pentecost of Peace" www.fatherjohndear.org, May 13, 2008.

*here has your reading of this book and* the words of John Dear led you? Some may be angry at the very thought of acting nonviolently in the face of hostility and aggression directed at us personally or nationally. That is not surprising; our culture conditions us to retaliate, to fight back, to defend our possessions and ourselves. Others may hear the message of active nonviolence with acceptance but wonder about how they might fulfill the call. A fervent few will take up the challenge of bringing active nonviolence to a world plagued by retaliation and war. Wherever you find yourself, accept yourself in that place. Yet you are encouraged not to remain there, wherever "there" may be. Through further reading, prayer for guidance and discussion with other people, allow yourself to grow in wisdom and action. A small sign hangs in my kitchen: "Please be patient. God's not finished with me yet." The Good News is that God is not yet finished with forming us into the people we were created to be.

Without question, for those who choose to follow Jesus along the path of active nonviolence, the way will not be easy. Sacrifice is required, perhaps the sacrifice of relationships with people you considered to be friends who will disagree with your view of nonviolence. The sacrifice of security may be called for before an era of peace emerges. John Dear's life and the lives of his mentors, Jesuit Daniel Berrigan, Mother Teresa, Dorothy Day, Mohandas Gandhi, the martyrs of Central America—all reveal the sacrifices they were called to make for the cause of peace. We must never forget that Jesus has already made the supreme sacrifice for us. His words as he faced death, prepared to die and met his followers after the Resurrection echo through the centuries: Peace be with you! Those who choose to follow Jesus along the path to peace will never walk alone. The Lord will be with you. Peace will be with you despite all appearances to the contrary.

Spirit of the Living God, shower us with your peace.
Spirit of the Living God, fill us with your courage.
Spirit of the Living God, may we forever praise your name.
Spirit of the Living God, send us forth to do your will.
Amen. Amen. Amen.

Suggested Services for Prayer Gatherings to Celebrate Peace

Each day of the year calls us to prayer. Particular days may arise that heighten our desire to shine God's light on historic and spiritual occasions. The following are sample prayer services, which focus on days of memory throughout the year. Use the sample service provided below as a starting point for your own services or for your own group. In using these suggestions, you will want to flesh out these ideas with words or actions pertinent to your group. (In *The God of Peace*, pp. 185–194, John Dear discusses "The Liturgy of Nonviolence: The Peace-making Community Worships the God of Peace.") Those creating prayer services may wish to refer to this resource. For homilies, create your own or go to www.fatherjohndear.org or use any of John's books to glean meaningful reflections. Or simply use any of the "Thoughts from John" already printed in this book.

Following the sample prayer service below is a list of other possible commemoration dates as well as suggested Scripture readings, possible homilies and songs for each day.

s a m p l e   p r a y e r   s e r v i c e
January 1: World Peace Day
Gathering Prayer: Loving God, we come to you at the birth of a new year with hearts eager to bring your peace to life on our planet. For the days and months to come we ask for the gifts of loving hearts to accept all your people, courage to follow you no matter what the cost and wisdom to determine your way of peace in a strife-riddled world. Peace we ask of you, O Lord, a way of peace that we might share with others. Amen.

Gathering Music: "Let There Be Peace on Earth" (*Gather,* 731)

Scripture Readings: Psalm 51:1–17; Matthew 7:1–5

Homily/Further Reading Suggestion: Read from www.FatherJohn Dear.org, Homilies, Jan. 1, 2004.

Reflection

Where does this time of prayer lead us in this new year of hope? What actions, personal and communal, do we feel called to carry out in the months to come?

Prayer: God...I shall fear no one. I shall place all my trust in You. I shall walk into the public world proclaiming my love for all people, especially the poor, resisting death and oppression and choosing life. I shall not be afraid. Jesus, I am coming. I will follow you. Receive me into your reign of love and peace. (from *Seeds of Nonviolence*, p. 147)

Vow of Nonviolence

Recognizing the violence in my own heart, yet trusting in the goodness and mercy of God, I vow to practice the nonviolence of Jesus who taught us in the Sermon on the Mount—

"Blessed are the peacemakers, they will be called the sons and daughters of God.... You have heard that it was said, love your neighbor and hate your enemy. But I say to you, Love your enemies and pray for those who persecute you that you may be sons and daughters of your God in heaven."

Before God the Creator and the Holy Spirit, I vow to carry out in my life the love and example of Jesus

—by striving for peace within myself and seeking to be a peace-maker in my daily life;

—by accepting suffering in the struggle for justice rather than inflicting it;

—by refusing to retaliate in the face of provocation and violence;

—by persevering in nonviolence of tongue and heart;

—by living conscientiously and simply so that I neither deprive others of the means to live or harm creation;

—by actively resisting evil and working nonviolently to abolish war and the causes of war from my own heart and from the face of the earth.

Closing Prayer: God, I trust in your sustaining love and believe that just as you gave me the grace and desire to offer this, so you will also bestow abundant grace to fulfill it.[1]

Closing Music: "Lord of All Nations, Grant Me Grace" (*Gather*, 634)

Notes

1 John Dear, *The Advent of the God of Peace: Reflections for Advent 2007* (Erie, Pa.: Pax Christi, 2007), p. 54.

other possible days to commemorate

Martin Luther King, Jr., Day

Gathering Music: "We Shall Overcome" (*Gather*, 724)

Gathering Prayer: God, help us to dedicate our lives to serving the poor by demanding justice and peace in nonviolent ways. May we accept suffering rather than inflict it on others. Show us how to make peace through persistent reconciliation and nonviolence. And may we lead the way to a world that will study war no more. Renew in us Dr. King's dream of a beloved community of humanity that brings hope for the future. Amen. (Adapted from *Seeds of Nonviolence*, p. 29)

Scripture Readings: 2 Chronicles 7:14; John 20:19–23

Homily/Further Reading Suggestion: "My Bible tells me that Good Friday comes before Easter Sunday," Martin Luther King, Jr., used to say. "To be a Christian," he said, "one must take up the cross, with all of its difficulties and agonizing and tension-packed content and carry it until that very cross leaves its marks upon us and redeems us to that more excellent way which comes only through suffering." On another occasion, King told a crowd of followers, "When I took up the cross, I recognized its meaning.... The cross is something you bear, and ultimately something that you die on.... Before the crown we wear there is the cross that we must bear. Let us bear it!" he declared. "Bear it for truth. Bear it for justice, and bear it for peace." (From *Seeds of Nonviolence*, p. 97)

Reflection: We each have a dream for ourselves. What is your dream? For yourself? The world? Spend some time dreaming that dream.

Closing Prayer: God, you see all that I am. You know my thoughts, my heart, what I say and what I do. I know you love me and I place my trust in you. Therefore, I do not fear any human being. I do not fear anything. I do not fear the power of death. Help me then to resist death and all the fears that bind human beings. Help me to break through human fear into true human relationships, into true solidarity with the poor and oppressed of the world, into voluntary poverty, into a deep, prayerful peace in my heart, into acts of nonviolence that can spark a transformation of the policies of death and oppression into food and housing for the poor. In the moment of confrontation, when I am publicly challenged, mocked or attacked, in those days ahead when I may be arrested and jailed for my nonviolent resistance, in those encounters when I embark on a new relationship with my oppressed sisters and brothers, in the hour of my death, let me pass from all fear to complete calm, peace, and trust rooted and grounded in you and your love. My daily prayer is: I shall fear no one. I shall place all my trust in you. I shall walk into the public world proclaiming my love for all people, especially, the poor, resisting death and oppression and choosing life. I shall not be afraid, Jesus, I am coming. I will follow you. Receive me into your reign of love and peace. *(From Seeds of Nonviolence, p. 147)*

Vow of Nonviolence (see p. 110)

Closing Music: "Voices That Challenge" (*Gather*, 721)

Ash Wednesday/Lent
Gathering Music: "Comfort, Comfort, O My People" (*Gather*, 326)

Gathering Prayer: O God, we come before you, humble in our waywardness, needing your forgiveness. Help us turn from any evil ways or any violence that lives within us. Clothe our being in spiritual sackcloth and ashes so that we may emerge from the lenten season cleansed by your forgiving love, ready to serve all creation actively in a spirit of nonviolence. Amen.

Scripture Readings: Joel 2:12–13; Psalm 77:1–3; Mark 12:41–44

Homily/Further Reading Suggestion: See John Dear "On the Road to Peace," www.NCRcafe.org February 5, 2008, vol. 2, number 22.

Reflection: How can you respond to God's request for our all? Where does this time of prayer lead us in the forty days of Lent in personal and communal action?

Closing Prayer: Hebrews 13:20–21

Vow of Nonviolence (see p. 110)

Closing Music: "Ashes" (*Gather*, 883)

August 6: Hiroshima/Nagasaki Memorial
Gathering Music: "For the Healing of the Nations" (*Gather*, 719)

Gathering Prayer: Forgiveness, forgiveness, forgiveness, Lord. We come seeking your forgiveness for violent acts of death and destruction in Hiroshima and Nagasaki decades ago. Though we did not make the decision to incinerate these cities and their people, we acknowledge that hostile thoughts and actions, then and now, by anyone contributes to fear and hatred in the world. Forgive our nation's past, and in the present and future guide leaders and citizens of all nations away from the use and terror of nuclear weapons. Amen.

Scripture Readings: Jeremiah 31:34; Psalm 117; Acts 13:38–39

Homily/Further Reading Suggestion: See John Dear's Hiroshima Day Speech at Los Alamos, August 9, 2005, published by www.CommonDreams.org.

Reflection: Where does this time of prayer lead us? What actions, personal and communal, do we feel called to carry out to prevent further violence in the world? Who will we invite to join us in the quest for peace?

Closing Prayer: Disarm me, God! Come, put away the sword I still carry somewhere in my heart. Take away the violence that lingers in my soul. Make me an instrument of Your peace. You have a plan for me: fulfill it! In this world of armaments, disarm me and I shall be able to disarm others. (From *Seeds of Nonviolence*, p. 146)

Vow of Nonviolence (see p. 110)

Closing Music: "World Peace Prayer" (*Gather*, 732)

September 11, 2001 Memorial

Gathering Music: "Make Me a Channel of Your Peace" (*Gather*, 726)

Gathering Prayer: Lord, we remember with broken hearts the day our lives as we had known them changed. We struggle to forgive, knowing we will not forget. Yet as we gather today we bring to you our desire to forgive those who did not truly know what they were doing as they obliterated thousands of human lives. We ask forgiveness for the thousands of lives that have been lost in retaliation. We offer you our future free of hatred, full of hope. May this day teach us to search for what made others hate our land and our culture so much. Where we discover our faults, make us instruments of change. We are your people. Help us to live that role in peace and nonviolence. Amen.

Scripture Readings: Numbers 14:19; Psalm 55:1–9, 22; 2 Corinthians 1:9–11

Homily/Further Reading Suggestion: See *Transfiguration*, pp. 223–224.

Reflection: Consider how your thoughts, prayers and actions have taken you since September 11, 2001. Are you a person of deeper peace? Of greater anger? Of active nonviolence? Where does this time of prayer lead us? What action, personal and communal, do we feel called to carry out to bring peace to the world?

Closing Prayer: Come, God. There is still a trace of war and madness in my veins. Purify me, O God, and I shall let loose disarmament in the world that will cause people to praise you freely. Purify me of all violence and I shall stand before the powers and principalities without fear and free those trapped in the structures of fear and violence. (From *Seeds of Nonviolence,* p. 146)

Vow of Nonviolence (see p. 110)

Closing Music: "Prayer of Peace" (*Gather,* 729)

November 9: Kristallnacht Remembered (The Beginning of the Holocaust)

Gathering Music: "God of Day and God of Darkness" (*Gather,* 761)

Gathering Prayer: O God, we gather to remember what happens when good people do nothing. Kristallnacht occurred within the space of a few hours yet ultimately led to the annihilation of more than six million people—your people, Lord. In remembering we ask you to keep us mindful of those who may seem to be different in race, culture, or sexual orientation in our day. Give us understanding hearts, wise minds and courage to work for peace when turmoil rises. And, please, Lord, continue to heal the survivors of the Holocaust. Amen.

Scripture Readings: Leviticus 19:17; Psalm 9:13–20; Luke 6:20–31

Homily/Further Reading Suggestion: Kristallnacht, the night of broken glass, was an event that spanned just two days November 9–10 in 1938. It marked the beginning of civilization's most brutal attack upon an entire people, the Jews. Jewish people in Nazi Germany and Austria were subjected to assault and the destruction of their homes and businesses, synagogues and cemeteries as hatred raced unbridled through the streets. People were hauled off to concentration camps, never to be seen by their families again. All because some considered them "different."

Reflection: What groups of people are persecuted in our own time, in our own country? How does this time of prayer guide us to reach out to them? What actions, personal and communal, might we initiate on their behalf in the name of peace and nonviolence? In the name of Jesus?

Closing Prayer: God, I beg You: give us your peace. Grant us your spirit that we may all repent from the ways of violence and convert to your Way of Nonviolence. (From *Seeds of Nonviolence*, p. 148)

Vow of Nonviolence (see p. 110)

Closing Music: "Bless the Lord, My Soul" (*Gather*, 141)

Thanksgiving

Gathering Music: "How Good It Is" (*Gather*, 727)

Gathering Prayer: Lord, we gather to give thanks for your many blessings to our country. We are mindful that the first Thanksgiving on America's shores was the peaceful gathering of peoples different in appearance, culture and faith. Yet they gathered and shared, respecting the otherness of the other. In our thankfulness for this day when we honor your blessings and gifts to us, may we reach out to others beyond our families, beyond our communities, beyond our borders in your spirit of love and compassion. We give you thanks and praise, O Lord God. Amen.

Scripture Readings: Isaiah 63:7 9; Colossians 3:12-17

Homily/Further Reading Suggestion: A Reading from the Mayflower Compact of 1620
IN THE NAME OF GOD, AMEN. We, whose names are underwritten, the Loyal Subjects of our dread Sovereign Lord King James, by the Grace of God.... Having undertaken for the Glory of God, and Advancement of the Christian Faith, and the Honour of our King and Country, a Voyage to plant the first

Colony in the northern Parts of Virginia; Do by these Presents, solemnly and mutually, in the Presence of God and one another, covenant and combine ourselves together into a civil Body Politick, for our better Ordering and Preservation, and Furtherance of the Ends aforesaid: And by Virtue hereof do enact, constitute, and frame, such just and equal Laws, Ordinances, Acts, Constitutions, and Officers, from time to time, as shall be thought most meet and convenient for the general Good of the Colony; unto which we promise all due Submission and Obedience. IN WITNESS whereof we have hereunto subscribed our names at Cape-Cod the eleventh of November...1620.

Reflection: Where does this time of shared prayer lead us? Our hearts are filled with thankfulness for the blessings of our land envisioned by our ancestors as the Mayflower Compact began "in the name of God." Yet history reminds us that all did not remain peaceful between the colonists and the indigenous people of the Americas. Settlers took the land that had been home to the Native Americans. They gave them diseases that the Native Americans had no immunity to resist. Skirmishes and wars separated various groups that had once been friends. What actions, both personal and communal, will we undertake to lead our country toward becoming a land of friendship, peace and harmony built on mutual respect for all people and love of God?

Closing Prayer: Empower me to give homes to the homeless, food to the foodless, love to the loveless, clothes to the clothesless, hope to the hopeless, peace to the peaceless. Inspire everyone to renounce their bourgeois lifestyles and turn to the suffering poor with the hand of peace.

Vow of Nonviolence (see p. 110)

Closing Music: "Bread for the World" (*Gather*, 827)

Advent/Christmas

Gathering Music: "Advent Gathering" (*Gather*, 324)

Gathering Prayer: O Lord of love, we prepare to enter the season of celebration of your birth on earth. That is a blessed occasion of long ago that we treasure in memory. Now is the time when we await your birth once again. We long for you to be reborn in our hearts. Your birth came in a tumultuous world of violence, yet the scene of your arrival is envisioned as one of peace and calm in the countryside of Bethlehem. As we await you, surround us with your peace. Guide us to become peacemakers in our own world of violence. We pray in your most holy name. Amen.

Scripture Reading: Isaiah 2:2–4; Psalm 27:1, 4, 13–14; Matthew 7:21, 24–27

Homily/Further Reading Suggestion: O Lord, peace seems so elusive because we live in fear: fear of loss, fear of pain and of death. We know you overcome these fears through your life and death and Resurrection. We search for the places where fear enters our lives. We accept your gift of healing peace.

The secular world begins the celebration of the Christmas season with shopping frenzies, advertisements telling us what every one of our friends and family wants and needs for Christmas gifts, what holiday celebrations we can't do without. We know these activities do not represent the true Advent or Christmas. They provide a façade of celebration that can obscure the deeper meaning. Now is the time to "shop" for Jesus as we seek him among the poor of our cities and countryside. Now is the time to "advertise" what Christmas means to us in its deepest sense. Now is the time to give gifts to those we do not know who hunger and thirst and feel they have little to celebrate. We might invite neighbors to attend religious services with us during the weeks to come. A holiday gathering might include reading Advent passages from Isaiah. We have the option to bring a truer meaning of Christmas into our secular world.

Reflection: Where does this time of prayer for the Advent coming of Jesus lead us? What actions, personal and communal, do we feel called to carry out in a culture where materialism has replaced the spiritual celebration of our Lord's birth?

Closing Prayer: Come, God. Disarm me without my knowing it, and then, show me that you are the Disarming One, nonviolent from the beginning of time until the end of time. Disarming Presence, Unconditional Love, Great Reconciler, Suffering Servant, Patience Personified, Peaceful Mother, come bearing peace. (From *Seeds of Nonviolence*, p. 146)

Vow of Nonviolence (see p. 110)

Closing Music: "Creator of the Stars of Night" (*Gather*, 337) appendix   b

Suggested Music for Prayer Gatherings to Celebrate Peace

[Selected from *Gather* (Chicago, Ill.: GIA, 1994)]

324   Advent Gathering
552   All the Earth, Proclaim God's Glory
820   All Who Hunger
690   Anthem
883   Ashes
759   At Evening
141   Bless the Lord, My Soul
659   Blest Are They
658   Bring Forth the Kingdom
827   Bread for the World
326   Comfort, Comfort, O My People
337   Creator of the Stars of Night
594   Dwelling Place
572   For the Beauty of the Earth
719   For the Healing of the Nations
583   Gifts That Last
761   God of Day and God of Darkness
882   Healer of Our Every Ill
727   How Good It Is
731   Let There Be Peace on Earth
634   Lord of All Nations, Grant Me Grace
726   Make Me a Channel of Your Peace
728   Peace Is Flowing Like a River
729   Prayer of Peace
80   [Psalm 85] Come, O Lord, and Set Us Free

Alperovitz, Gar. *The Decision to Use the Atomic Bomb.* New York: Knopf, 1995.

Barber, Elinore, et al. *Moral Leadership: A Resource for the Theological Exploration of Vocation at Hastings College,* vol. 3, Fall. Hastings, Neb.: Hastings College, 2005.

Dear, John. *The Advent of the God of Peace: Reflections for Advent 2007.* Erie, Pa: Pax Christi, 2007.

———. *Disarming the Heart: Toward a Vow of Nonviolence.* Scottsdale, Pa.: Herald, 1993.

———. *The God of Peace: Toward a Theology of Nonviolence.* Eugene, Oreg.: Wipf and Stock, 1994.

———. *Jean Donovan and the Call to Discipleship.* Erie, Pa.: Pax Christi, 2005.

———. *Jesus the Rebel: Bearer of God's Peace and Justice.* Lanham, Md.: Sheed and Ward, 2000.

———. *Living Peace: A Spirituality of Contemplation and Action.* New York: Image, 2001.

———. *Mary of Nazareth: Prophet of Peace.* Notre Dame, Ind.: Ave Maria, 2003.

———. ed., *Mohandas Gandhi: Essential Writings.* Maryknoll, N.Y.: Orbis, 2002.

———. *Oscar Romero and the Nonviolent Struggle for Justice.* Erie, Pa.: Pax Christi, 2004.

———. *Our God is Nonviolent.* Cleveland: Pilgrim, 1990.

———. *Peace Behind Bars: A Peacemaking Priest's Journal from Jail.* Franklin, Wis.: Sheed and Ward, 1999.

———. *A Persistent Peace: One Man's Struggle for a Nonviolent World.* Chicago: Loyola, 2008.

————. *Put Down Your Sword.* Grand Rapids, Mich.: Eerdmans, 2008.

————. *The Questions of Jesus:Challenging Ourselves to Discover Life's Great Answers..* New York: Image, 2004.

————. *The Sacrament of Civil Disobedience.* Baltimore: Fortkamp, 1994.

————. *Seeds of Nonviolence.* Eugene, Or.: Wipf and Stock, 2006.

————. *The Sound of Listening: A Retreat Journal from Thomas Merton's Hermitage.* New York: Continuum, 1999.

————. *Transfiguration: A Meditation on Transforming Ourselves and Our World.* New York: Image, 2007.

———— and William Hart McNichols. *You Will Be My Witnesses: Saints, Prophets and Martyrs.* Maryknoll, N.Y.: Orbis, 2006.

Normile, Patti. *Prayers for Caregivers.* Cincinnati: St. Anthony Messenger Press, 1995.

web sites

An extensive list of Web sites may be found at www.johndear.org in "Links."

www.americancatholic.org

www.catholicworker.org

www.forusa.org

www.franciscanresources.com

www.interfaithpathstopeace.org

www.johndear.org

www.mertoninstitute.org

www.NCRcafe.org

www.paxchristi.org

www.peacefultomorrows.org [September Eleventh Families for Peaceful Tomorrows]

www.sandamianofoundation.org
www.sojo.net
www.VAIW.ORG [Iraq Veterans Against the War]

f i l m s
The Narrow Path, The San Damiano Foundation,
www.sandamianofoundation.org.

o t h e r   w o r k s   e d i t e d   b y   j o h n   d e a r
And the Risen Bread: Selected Poems of Daniel Berrigan, 1957–1997. New
   York: Fordham University Press, 1998.
Apostle of Peace: Essays in Honor of Daniel Berrigan. Maryknoll, N.Y.:
   Orbis, 1996.
Christ Is with the Poor: Stories and Sayings of Horace McKenna. Available
   from The McKenna Center for the Homeless, Washington, D.C.
*It's a Sin to Build a Nuclear Weapon: The Collected Works on War and
   Christian Peacemaking of Richard McSorley, s.j.* Baltimore:
   Fortkamp, 1991.
The Road to Peace: Writings on Peace and Justice by Henry Nouwen.
   Maryknoll, N.Y.: Orbis, 1998.
*The Vision of Peace: Faith and Hope in Northern Ireland by Nobel Peace
   Laureate, Mairead Corrigan Maguire.* Maryknoll, N.Y.: Orbis, 1999.

topical index

energy of peace, 59–66
  concluding prayers on, 65–66
  reflections on, 64
  Scripture on, 64–65
enmity, 12, 46
Esquivel, Adolfo Perez, 20
evil
  concluding prayers on, 58
  Dear on, 53–56
  facing, with love, 51–58
  reflections on, 57
  Scripture on, 57
examen, 63
eye-for-an-eye, 68

F
fear, 27–28
  God and, 28
  Jesus and, 26, 56
  nuclear weapons and, 90
  violence and, 26
Fellowship of Reconciliation, xv
felonies, xvi
Flight 93, 79
"For the Beauty of the Earth," 119
"For the Healing of the Nations,"
  119
forgiveness, 60
  King on, 62
Francis of Assisi, Saint, xiii, xx, 36, 85
Franciscans, 70
freedom
  of press, 34
  of speech, 34

G
Galilee, xvii–xviii, 98

Gandhi, Mahatma, 25, 59, 82, 106
  assassination of, 27
  on nonviolence, 27–28
  on prayer, 46
Garden of Gethsemane, xii
Gaudium et Spes, 81
General Assembly, 93
General Hospital (television show), xiii
gentleness, 25–32
  Dear on, 27–30
  defining, 25–26
  reflection questions, 30
  Scripture on, 30
Germany, 77
"Gifts That Last," 119
God, vii, xiv
  fear and, 28
  Jesus and, 91
  love of, 12, 46, 55
  meeting, 92
  mercy of, 37
  nonviolence and, 44
  peace and, 4, 47, 70, 80, 81
  sins and, 96
"God of Day and God of Darkness,"
  114, 119
The God of Peace (Dear), 107
Graduate Theological Union in
  California, xv
grassroots movements, 81
Great Britain, 77
Greyda, Umm, 20
Ground Zero, 29, 97. *See also*
  September 11, 2001
Gulf War, 20
Gumbleton, Thomas, xv

scripture index